X
X rcta

THE COLLEGE of West Anglia
Landbeach Road • Milton • Cambridge
Tel: (01223) 860701

2

THE COLLEGE OF WEST ANGLIA
LEARNING CENTRE

The Illustrated Guide to

DOGS

The Illustrated Guide to
DOGS

by
LUDEK DOBRORUKA

Illustrated by
ZDENEK BERGER

TREASURE PRESS

NOTE TO READER
The cropping of dog's ears is an
illegal practice in the UK, although it
is carried out in other parts of
Europe.

0727768

(m) 626.71 D

Translated by Olga and Ivan Kuthan
Line drawings by Zdeněk Berger
Graphic design by Eva Adamcová
Designed and produced by Aventinum for
Treasure Press,
Michelin House, 81 Fulham Road
London SW 3, 6RB

Copyright © 1990 Aventinum, Prague

All Rights Reserved.
No part of this publication may be reproduced or transmitted
in any form or by any means, electronic or mechanical,
including photocopying, recording or any information storage
and retrieval system, without permission in writing from the
copyright owner.

ISBN 1 85051 509 3

Printed in Czechoslovakia by Svoboda
3/15/25/51-01

CONTENTS

THE DOG – OUR FRIEND AND HELPER

After years of debate experts more or less agree that the domestic dog is descended from the wolf. Many theories have been put forward to explain our ancestors' domestication of the dog but there is no evidence to support any of them. It is difficult even for an experienced archaeologist or zoologist to determine whether fossil remains are those of a wolf or a dog. Initially, the two probably differed more in behaviour than appearance. Attempts at domestication evidently took place in many parts of the northern hemisphere, quite independently of each other and at various times.

The oldest archaeological finds which may be interpreted as the remains of dogs have been unearthed in Asia, Europe and, interestingly enough, in North America. These finds are from Cayönü in Turkey (9500 BC), Star Carr in Scotland (*circa* 7500 BC) and Lemhi County, Idaho (*circa* 9000 BC). We do not know what these dogs looked like nor how they were used by people at that time.

More precise information is gleaned from various depictions of the dog in the ancient cultures of the Orient and Egypt. Anatolian wall paintings, Palestinian rock paintings and Persian vases from the seventh to the fourth millennium BC show mainly hunting dogs. Around 3500 BC shepherds in the Sahara Desert, whose many rock drawings have survived to this day, used the dog primarily to help tend and guard grazing sheep and to a small degree also for hunting. In northern Europe dogs were used to pull sleds, as proved by archaeological finds dating from the sixth to the fourth millennium BC. Of interest is the fact that in the second millennium BC dogs in Crete were harnessed to ploughs.

From time immemorial dogs were evidently also used by people against people. Evidence of this is found, for example, on a silver Phoenician bowl from an Etruscan tomb in Italy, depicting dogs hunting what are probably slaves.

Before long people apparently began some kind of selective breeding. From the original primitive dogs, which resembled the wolf, people selected those individuals which, in one way or another, suited their needs and, through careful breeding, fixed their specific characteristics. Around 3000 BC, for example, dogs with drooping ears appeared on the scene; Egyptian reliefs from *circa* 2000 BC show short-legged and dwarf dogs; depictions from *circa* 2000 BC show dogs which exhibit a fair resemblance to Pinschers. Large, mastiff-like dogs were used in hunting as well as in battle in India and Mesopotamia in the third to the first milennia BC.

The first handbook on dog breeding, which lists their proper characteristics and flaws and which also gives instructions on how to proceed when mating a bitch, as well as listing the various aids for training a dog, was written by Xenophon (430–352 BC). Since that time many books have been written on the subject of breeding and rearing dogs. Various new breeds were developed and others became extinct but, regardless of their social status, people have always retained an interest in dogs. Nowadays there is a steady increase in the number of people for whom their dog is not only a helper but first and foremost a friend and companion.

BEFORE ACQUIRING A DOG

There are many reasons why you might decide to own a dog. Whatever reason you have for acquiring a dog, however, do so only after careful consideration and after weighing all the pros and cons; only then will you and the dog be happy together. The dog is an animal which is closely tied to the company of a pack and you will be taking the place of the pack. The dog must regard you as its pack leader, a being who knows what is right, who makes the decisions, metes out punishment and rewards, is just and is loved. You will be taking on the responsibility for your new companion. You must bring up your dog and train it, see to its well being, give it time and attention, let it out several times a day, walk it, brush it and feed it.

Prepare yourself for the fact that you will also have to cover various expenses (inoculation fees, etc.) and that you may possibly have to face the animosity of people in your neighbourhood who do not like dogs. You must look after the dog when it is ill, and take into account that it will grow old and will no longer be able to fulfil all your wishes but will continue to love you and depend on you as before. You are taking upon yourself a considerable responsibility for a period of ten to fifteen years; if you still really want a dog go ahead and get one, armed with the knowledge that you must never fail it.

People often ask whether they should choose a purebred dog or a mongrel. Every dog has a personality of its own just like people. A mongrel may be just as friendly, faithful, courageous, timid or disobedient as a purebred dog. If you decide in favour of a pedigree dog, however, you have the guarantee that its talents and temperament will be broadly in line with those of the respective breed, and you can also predict what the puppy will look like when it is fully grown. Furthermore, if, for example, you wish to breed a litter out of a purebred bitch you will know beforehand what the puppies will be like and will find it easier to place them in good homes.

In the case of mongrels, you always run a certain risk. In my time I have seen many delightful puppies which the owners found they did not like at all once they were fully grown. Likewise, you cannot predict what kind of character such a dog will have. Of course, a mongrel may still be a dear companion and friend, although its appearance does not conform to the standard for any known breed. If you decide to take on the risks involved in the acquisition of a mongrel you must not forget that your duty and responsibility will be just as great as in the case of a pedigree dog.

Naturally everyone likes one breed more than another. Before acquiring a dog of a definite breed, however, consider whether the character of the breed suits your taste and lifestyle and whether you will be able to satisfy the dog's requirements. If you acquire a Greyhound, for instance, you must provide it with plenty of exercise; Poodles and some terriers require regular and relatively demanding care of their coats; it would be foolish to acquire a Neapolitan Mastiff where there are children or an Irish Wolfhound if you have a one-room flat. Some breeds are quiet, others bark a lot; some have unalterable hunting instincts, others would not even consider chasing a hare; some are friendly to everyone, others are suspicious of strangers; some are simply made to be household pets, whereas others would be miserable if they were housebound.

This book will help you to decide. It depicts 170 breeds and provides basic information about each (e.g. the height and weight of the dog, the various possible colourings of each breed, character traits and the uses to which it has traditionally been put). The history of each breed is also given, as well as practical advice as regards grooming. If you find a breed to your liking you would be well advised to visit several dog shows where you can supplement your theoretical knowledge with direct impressions of the living dog.

There are about 500 different breeds of dog worldwide, including those which are still waiting to receive international recognition. The Federation Cynologique Internationale (FCI), founded in 1911, requires that respective countries specify the standards for the breeds which originated in those countries. FCI has also worked out the basic grouping of breeds according to their relationship and according to their use. This basic grouping is naturally modified in various countries according to local needs and on the basis of exhibition practices. In France and Italy, for example, hounds are divided into several groups; in Sweden spitzes are recognised as a separate group, etc.

This book observes the following basic grouping:

Working dogs

All breeds included in this group have developed from dogs which helped herdsmen with their cattle and sheep thousands of years ago. They can be further divided into mountain dogs and other sheepdogs. Mountain dogs have a strain of Mastiff blood in them because they needed to be strong, courageous dogs which would stand up to wolves and bears. In later times most sheep-herding breeds were trained to keep the herds together and prevent them from wandering. They had to be independent and able to act on their own initiative. That is why many sheepdog breeds also became good guard and utility dogs.

Utility dogs

The ancestry of the breeds included in this group is extremely varied. Common to all is that they were trained in times past to defend property and to fight. Their number, however, also includes breeds that were 'jacks of all trades' – they guarded, helped in hunting, carried burdens, pulled sleds.

Terriers

The name of this group is derived from the Latin word *terra*, meaning earth, and indicates that these were originally dogs used to drive or dig badgers and foxes from their lairs. Such work demands independent, sturdy, courageous dogs of small to medium size. Because of their outstanding qualities, terriers were crossed with other breeds, particularly hounds, thereby giving rise to terrier breeds suitable for other work.

Hounds

The characteristic common to the dogs of this group is that they pursue game, prevent its escape, and give sportsmen the opportunity to kill it. The way the dog goes about its work, however, differs according to the type of breed. Some breeds track the game slowly, others pursue the game in packs with loud barking and either bring it down or chase it towards huntsmen waiting with guns.

Gundogs, retrievers and spaniels

All gundogs evolved from the hounds. As early as the sixth century BC, the Greek historian Xenophon mentions hounds which, instead of pursuing game, stood completely still with head held high when sniffing a scent. Originally this behaviour was considered undesirable, but later such dogs were used to help in netting birds and in falconry. This group also includes the French Epagneuls and German Wachtelhund, which represent a kind of bridge between the hounds and the gundogs.

British sportsmen made specialists of their gundogs, i.e. pointers and setters. These must sniff a scent rapidly and from afar and mark the spot where the game is located. They must not bring in the downed game – that is the job of the retriever. Chasing game out of impenetrable, thick undergrowth is the work of trackers — spaniels. Some breeds are kept only by sportsmen, but most of the dogs in this group are also excellent companions, so their uses are many.

Toy dogs

Toy dogs have one characteristic in common – they are all very small. Many of them look like miniature versions of larger breeds. These dogs can appear very fragile and delicate, but most are surprisingly robust and playful, many make excellent watchdogs and some have fairly keen hunting instincts. Most are kept as companion dogs.

BUYING A PUPPY

When buying a puppy, always get it from a reliable breeder because then you can be sure the dog will be healthy. If you are a first-time owner, it is a good idea to take an experienced dog owner with you who can advise you on selecting a pup. It is not always easy to choose the best from a litter of six- to eight-week-old puppies.

A puppy is taken from its mother only after it is weaned. Generally this is at the age of seven to eight weeks. A reliable breeder will certainly not give you a puppy before this age. It is a good thing if you can see the bitch, and possibly also the sire, before buying a puppy, for you can often tell more from this than from studying the pedigree. The bitch, especially, often passes on her temperament to her pups. Do not buy a pup from a nervous, timid or aggressive bitch. The pedigree, of course, is a very important document as you will appreciate if you yourself become a breeder. Moreover, without a pedigree you cannot enter your dog in many dog shows, trials and other canine events.

Dog or bitch

Think twice about whether to buy a dog or a bitch. A dog generally has a stronger personality than a bitch and thus is usually more difficult to train. When he is fully grown he will want to put his scent (urine) on various objects and you will find it difficult to train him not to urinate on shrubs, small trees and taller herbaceous plants in the garden. (This does very little harm, however.) Also, when bitches in your neighbourhood are on heat, a dog may become restless, may even try to run off to find the bitch, may scratch at doors, stop eating, howl, and so on.

A bitch is usually more docile and therefore more easily trained and handled. She does not put her scent on objects, although if allowed to urinate on a lawn, she may cause patches of grass to turn brown. However, twice a year she will be on heat. At this time her scent will attract male dogs which will attempt to enter the garden where the bitch lives, or perhaps even camp out on the doorstep of your home. When you go for walks at this time you must keep her on a tight lead and away from the dogs that will try to mate with her. If you do not wish your bitch to come into season (on heat) or to have pups, you can have her spayed. Spayed bitches tend to get fat very easily.

The above points cover the more extreme possibilities of each sex. Naturally, they are not always the rule, but it is a good thing to keep them in mind.

Choosing a pup

When choosing a dog, watch the pups in the litter closely and for a long time. You will see that one pup is livelier than the others, that some are bold, while others are timid. Observe how they behave, for instance when exposed to loud noises, whether they are watchful or easily startled. Do not take an excessively timid, nervous or aggressive pup. Then make your choice according to which personality suits you best. Ask the breeder if the pups have already been wormed and what medicine was used. The worming cure must be repeated after a certain time and so you must know both when it was last given and what dosage was used. In some breeds the tail is normally docked. This is generally done a few days after birth. In the UK it is not permitted to crop dogs' ears.

Nowadays effective vaccination is given against many dangerous contagious diseases. As a rule pups are vaccinated after they are three months old; in some cases provisional vaccination can be given from the fifth week onwards. Ask the breeder or your vet to give you all necessary information on this. A certificate is given for each vaccination.

Ask what food the puppy has been accustomed to and in what amounts.

For the first few days you must keep to this diet. Altering the food at the same time as making a change in environment may lead to serious digestive upsets. If you intend to change the diet in some way you must introduce these changes very gradually and only begin to do so when the puppy feels absolutely at home and is eating well.

Check, preferably with the aid of an experienced breeder or dog owner, whether the characteristics evident in the pup correspond to the breed standard (bite, coloration, etc.). In some breeds certain characteristics change with age. Find out about this before deciding definitely on your choice of breed.

Bringing the puppy home

Before bringing the puppy home, you must see to it that everything is in readiness for its arrival so that it will quickly become accustomed to its new surroundings. At first you must keep the puppy indoors, even if the grown dog will later be kept in a kennel in the garden. The puppy must have a place of its own where it will sleep and can go for peace and quiet. All dogs like to have something above their heads and so it is recommended that the dog's bed is in an enclosed, roofed-over spot, although this is not essential. A small mattress that is not too soft and is covered with washable fabric makes good bedding. For small companion dogs you can buy suitable baskets in a pet shop. You can also purchase basic equipment, such as a lead and collar. Do not forget to buy or provide a toy for your pup – pet shops offer a wide assortment. By doing this you will greatly limit the pup's attempts at gnawing various objects in the household.

Other indispensable aids are the articles neded for the care of your dog's coat. A clean, well-groomed dog does credit to its owner. It also smells less and will be free from parasites. At first you will require a brush and comb, which you can later supplement according to need and according to your dog's coat type. Small puppies should not be bathed; even later on baths should be kept to a minimum so that the dog's coat does not lose its natural oil unnecessarily, thereby becoming dry and brittle. Use a mild soap or special dog shampoo. After bathing, the dog should be dried well with a towel or electric hair-drier and allowed to run about to keep warm.

Dog baskets

Signs of health

You should be aware of the normal attributes of a healthy dog:

body temperature (rectal): 38–39 °C (in some breeds, e.g. hairless dogs, 42 °C)

pulse (heartbeats per minute)

puppy (up to one year of age):	110–120
full-grown dog:	90–100
old dog (from about the age of seven):	70–80

respiration (breaths per minute at rest)

puppy:	18–20
full-grown dog:	16–18
old dog:	14–18

If you have any doubts about the health of your dog, consult a vet. It is recommended that you choose one who will tend your dog from the very beginning and, knowing it well, will be able to give you the best advice.

UNDERSTANDING YOUR DOG

The dog's natural characteristics, which were the basic precondition for its domestication, likewise govern its association with people. First and foremost here is the behaviour which makes life possible within a pack; in other words the dog's ability to subordinate itself to an individual who is higher up in the social order.

You will bring the new puppy home when it is about two months old. At this point of its development it is at a stage when young animals quickly and indelibly learn certain vitally important things. This is known as imprinting. You will be imprinted in the puppy's mind as its pack leader and your home as its environment; it will adapt to its new surroundings much more easily and quickly at this age than if it were older.. For the first two months you need not teach the dog anything except to respect the word 'no' and its name. You can also begin house training. Apart from that just see that it has plenty to eat, plenty of sleep, lots of human company, plays a lot and has plenty of exercise. After two months it may be gradually taught to come when called, walk on a lead and sit and lie down on command. If you want your dog merely to be a companion then that is probably all it needs to know. Remember certain important rules. Always talk to your dog in a quiet tone; a loud command should be the first degree of punishment. Constantly shouting at the dog will blunt its perception, but will not improve its obedience. Commands must be brief, clear and always expressed in the same words. Only then can you be sure that the dog will understand them. It is not certain whether a dog always recognises the words themselves, but it definitely registers the rhythm and cadence of your speech. It is a good idea to accompany each command with a specific gesture, so that later the dog will be able to obey your commands without words and from a greater distance. Praise the dog and pat it when it obeys your command. Punish it only when absolutely necessary and never harshly. The first degree of punishment is a loud voice. The dog readily recognises the change of tone and the raised voice tells it that it has done something wrong. The next degree of punishment may be a light slap with a twig, or better yet with a folded newspaper. Both make a characteristic sound that will be connected in the dog's mind with the fact that it did something wrong. Later it will suffice merely to rustle the newspaper without touching the dog. Never, under any circumstances, should you hit the dog with your hand or with the lead. These are objects in which it must always have absolute faith!

Your first early task will probably be to house-train the puppy. Here you must remember three rules: never be harsh with the puppy; any punishment must be administered immediately after the misdeed (it is senseless to administer it several minutes later as the puppy will not then connect cause with effect); never push the puppy's nose in the puddle it has made. This is cruel, unhygienic and has no positive effect. Observe your dog constantly. If it begins running about restlessly or whining, if it starts to look around for a rug or some other soft material, you must pick it up immediately, take it out of doors and be lavish with your praise if it relieves itself there. Naturally, at first you may not notice the signals being made by the puppy and it will relieve itself indoors. In that case pick it up at once, show it the puddle, scold it sharply and take it out of doors. At the beginning the puppy will relieve itself very often — twenty or more times a day. At this early stage it is best to keep the puppy confined to one room where there are many sheets of newspaper on the floor. If you succeed in noticing and putting it out in time at least five times in one day, you may hope that your efforts to house-train it will be successful. Observe your dog out of doors as well. Praise it and show how pleased you are whenever it relieves itself. Progress in its training should be evident within a week, and after three weeks the dog should indicate of its own accord that it wants to be let out. Try to accustom the dog to being let out at definite times.

Obedience is generally learned by the puppy more quickly. Be generous with your praise when your dog comes to you. Praise it even if you have previously been calling it in vain and were angry when it did not obey. A dog must want to come to its owner because it will be rewarded with praise, not punishment. If it does not want to obey, put it on a long lead and let it run about. Then, every time you call it, pull it towards you – without undue force, of course, for that would put the dog off. Then praise it and be nice to it. Later let it run free and try calling it from a short distance. In all probability you will be successful, particularly if you squat down when you call, for the dog knows that that is the position in which you usually play with it.

Walking a dog on a lead is another object of training. Lead the dog close to your left foot. Whenever it tries to run off or to strain at the lead, give it a short, sharp upwards tug, accompanied, perhaps, by a sharp reprimand. The dog will quickly learn to walk properly on a lead. If you have problems with a dog which pulls constantly, try using a choke chain. This must be put on and used correctly, with a sharp upwards pull which is then released.

This book does not deal with more complicated forms of training, such as the training of hunting or working dogs. There are numbers of specialist handbooks on these subjects and you can also get in touch with one of the many existing specialist organisations, where experts will advise you on all the various aspects of training your particular breed.

Canine expressions

If you want to be really good friends with your dog then you must learn to understand it. The dog, being a pack animal, has a given place in the social order of the pack, and this order is maintained by means of various signs and signals. Observe your dog carefully and notice its posture (the position of the individual parts of its body). For example, the ears are held in one way when the dog is fawning on its owner, but in a different way when it sees or senses something suspicious, and in a different way again when attacking. Observe how the dog bares its teeth: if it bares its teeth with its nose wrinkled, this is a threat; if it does not wrinkle its nose, but draws the corners of its mouth back, this is an expression of fear or uncertainty.

Many things can be expressed by the position and movements of the tail. Everybody knows what it means when a dog wags its tail or when it tucks it between its legs. The most important gestures for self-preservation in a pack are the gestures of superiority and subordination. Even in the roughest of fights, if one dog shows a sign of subordination, the fight will usually be over.

Facial expression: 1, threat; 2, uncertain threat; 3, weak threat; 4, faint threat (the dog is very uncertain); 5, fear; 6, expression of uncertainty in the presence of a dog of superior rank

16

Members of the same species do not usually fight to the death. For the victor it is usually enough for its adversary to admit its position of inferiority. In the wild there are very few exceptions to this rule — of which the human being, unfortunately, is one.

Wild carnivores of the canine family mark the territory they inhabit with their scent. These signs indicate to other canines, as well as to members of the animal's own pack, the territorial boundaries that must be respected by them. As a rule, canines mark their territories with urine. Domestic male dogs like to urinate on conspicuous or protruding objects in their surroundings and will carefully sniff these objects to determine who else has passed this way. Naturally the dogs who place their marks first are the males highest in the social order. The higher a mark is placed on an object the greater is the maker's standing. That is why dogs try to urinate as high up as possible. Naturally the dog must be sparing with his urine so as to be able to mark as many objects as possible and that is why he often releases only a few drops.

Besides visual signs (perceived with the eye) and olfactory signs (perceived with the sense of smell) dogs also use acoustic signs – perceived with the ear. These, however, are of far less importance. Whining and growling, for example, are used mainly by puppies to express various feelings of satisfaction and dissatisfaction. They are responded to on the one hand by the mother, and on the other hand by the other pups in the litter. Barking and howling make it possible for dogs to establish contact over greater distances.

Body language: 1, a self-confident, dominant animal in the presence of another dog; 2, threat; 3, trying to impress (tail wags from side to side); 4, unconcerned attitude; 5, uncertain threat; 6, posture when eating; 7, subordinate attitude; 8, uncertainty between threat and defence; 9, 10, 11, subordinate attitudes in the presence of a dog of superior rank

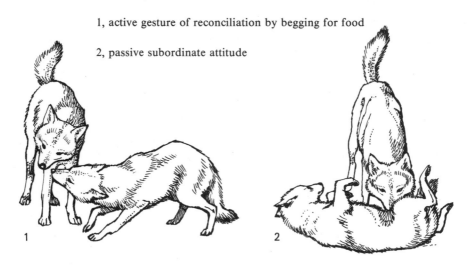

1, active gesture of reconciliation by begging for food

2, passive subordinate attitude

1

2

By observing your dog carefully you can learn much and begin to understand its language. For example, watch a bitch with her puppies and observe how she teaches them obedience. You will discover, for instance, that the severest punishment is when she grasps a puppy by the scruff of the neck and shakes it. Try it sometime with your own puppy (only, of course, if it does actually deserve this severest of punishments!) and you will see how effective it is.

CARE OF THE DOG

We have already discussed how to feed a new puppy when you bring it home. From the second to third month feed it five times a day, from the third to the fifth month four times a day, and from the fifth to the ninth month three times a day. Puppies older than nine months should be fed twice a day. Dogs of most breeds are fully grown in height around one year of age, but their mental and physical development still continues. Therefore, although one-year-old, as well as older, dogs may be fed only once a day, if possible it is preferable to give them two meals a day. As a guideline a dog weighing 10 kg should be given 650 g of food daily, one weighing 20 kg about 1 kg of food daily, and one weighing 50 kg about 2 kg of food daily.

Dogs are basically carnivores, but this does not mean that they should be fed nothing but meat. For a dog to remain healthy it should be fed equal proportions of meat and cereal (in the form of biscuit or cooked rice, oatmeal, etc.), with the addition of raw or cooked vegetables, and the occasional egg, piece of cheese and cooked fish (with the bones removed). This diet will ensure that the dog receives all the proteins, carbohydrates, fats, minerals, vitamins and roughage it requires.

Do make sure that the meat or offal you feed to your dog is not too fatty and has been produced under hygienic conditions. It should not be a minced up mixture of butcher's scrapings and unsaleable odds and ends which would otherwise end up in the bin.

Meat can be fed raw or cooked. Although cooking will remove some vitamins and alter the structure of protein, it will also ensure that harmful bacteria, worm eggs, etc., are killed off.

These days many households feed their pets on commercially prepared tinned or dried dog food. These products are usually excellent in their quality and standard of hygienic preparation and contain the right balance of all the proteins, fats, vitamins and minerals your dog will need. Tinned dog meat should be fed with a mixer biscuit in the proportions and quantity indicated on the can or packet label. Dried food should be given to the dog with the addition of a little gravy or warm water to moisten it, bring out its full flavour and aid digestion.

In addition to these foods, any family meal leftovers will make a tasty addition to the dog's dinner. These scraps can include meat, vegetables or pasta, but should not include anything sugary or fatty.

Be careful about feeding milk to an adult dog. It can cause diarrhoea and tummy upsets. Cheese is an excellent source of calcium and should prove very acceptable.

If your dog does develop diarrhoea, try adding a little dry bran to its food. If the diarrhoea persists, consult your vet.

Make sure that a bowl of fresh water is always available, especially when feeding dried foods or biscuits. Change the water a couple of times a day, even if it has not been drunk.

Avoid giving your dog any small bones, such as poultry bones or chop bones. These can splinter and cause choking. The best kind of bone is a large, raw shank bone with a knuckle end. Chewing this will help to keep the dog's teeth and gums healthy. If you are concerned at the possible mess caused by a real bone, you can buy a hard, chewy, bone substitute at a pet shop.

Accommodation

The dog must have its bed in a fixed place where it knows it can rest and sleep. Large breeds, working or hunting dogs, which cannot be kept indoors, are best housed in an enclosure in a yard or garden. The enclosure should be roomy and the fencing, or preferably wire netting, should be sufficiently high and provided with a base that will prevent any dog digging its way out under it. The ground area must be easy to clean and well drained, or, better yet, provided with a hard, slightly sloping surface so that water can run off. The enclosure must be located in a quiet, sheltered spot which is shaded from the sun during the hottest part of the day.

It must contain a kennel that will give shelter to the dog in bad weather. The walls, generally of wood, should be made of tongue-and-groove-fitted boards so that there are no draughty chinks. Best of all are double walls with good insulation between them. The kennel should not be placed directly on the ground but on a raised base or foundation. The best type of roof is one that can be removed or raised, allowing for easier cleaning of the interior and for ventilation on hot days. The inside space should be suitable for the size of

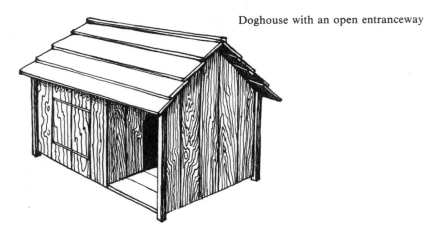

Doghouse with an open entranceway

the dog and allow it to lie down in comfort. If it is properly dimensioned the dog's own body heat will suffice to keep it warm. It is a good idea to provide the kennel with an entrance which will not only give additional protection in bad weather but will also be a welcome place to spend the night in hot weather. Some dogs do not tolerate any bedding in the kennel, but bedding will prevent a heavy dog from developing callouses on its elbows.

Grooming

Care must be devoted to the dog's coat, which is composed of several types of hairs. The outer coat is composed of long, straight or slightly wavy hairs called primary hairs. The undercoat is composed of secondary hairs and wool hairs. In some breeds these types of hair may be absent or modified. Generally, however, a dog's coat is composed of all the different types of hairs in more or less equal proportion. This coat composition resembles the coats of most wild canines.

If the undercoat is reduced and the outer coat is shorter, then the respective breed is called short-haired or smooth-haired. If the outer coat is longer, then the breed is called silky-haired. The primary hairs may also become coarser and, generally, at the same time wavy — such dogs are referred to as rough-haired or wire-haired. In Schnauzers, however, which are rough-haired, the primary hairs are not wavy.

The dog's coat does not grow at a regular pace, but only during certain periods, interrupted by periods of rest. Specialised organs are the tactile guard hairs which grow primarily on the head and are sensitive to the touch.

Caring for the hair of short-haired dogs is relatively simple. All it needs is brushing with a semi-hard brush or combing with a comb that is not too fine-toothed.

Long-haired breeds require greater care. Their coats must be thoroughly combed at least twice a week to prevent possible matting. Be careful merely to comb the hair, taking care not to pull any out or damage its structure. Use a comb with long, widely spaced, blunt teeth and pay particular attention to the backs of the ears, the inner thighs, the hair on the neck around the collar, the lower thighs, and the tail where the hair most often becomes matted. Having combed the dog, take a brush with hard, long, widely spaced bristles and brush the coat, first of all against the grain and then from the head to the hind-quarters.

For some rough-haired breeds, such as terriers, the breed standard specifies the correct form of the coat which gives the breed its typical shape and appearance. The coat is dealt with either by clipping or stripping. The method used is dependent on the texture of the coat as laid down by the standard, and the various tools used include dog clippers, stripping knives, scissors and metal combs. A rough-haired dog may be trimmed only when its coat is ready for it, i.e. when it begins to moult. This is done stage by stage so that it reaches the length required by the standard at exactly the right time for the show. The 'hairdressing' of rough-haired dogs is an art that you will acquire only through practice. If you are not preparing to show your dog, merely brush and comb its coat in the usual way.

Ears

Dogs with drop ears, mainly the long-haired breeds, require that special attention be paid to the ears. These must be cleaned regularly with a cotton-wool pad. Dogs which work in water require particular care as unpleasant ear infections are often caused by water entering the ear canal.

Nails

The dog's nails do not require any care if the dog has enough exercise out of doors. If, however, the nails click when the dog walks on a hard surface, they must be shortened. If you wish to do this yourself, trim the nails with special nail clippers, taking care to cut off only the tip so as not to damage the nerve. In the case of extremely hard nails it sometimes helps to soak them for five to ten minutes in warm soapy water. You can also have your dog's nails clipped at a special dog beauty parlour or by your vet.

Teeth

Sometimes a brownish encrustation, called tartar, forms on the teeth. This is usually removed by the dog itself if it is given the right food to chew on, e.g. a bone, hard biscuits and the like. If necessary the teeth can be cleaned with canine toothpaste and a soft toothbrush. The toothpaste can be obtained from your vet. Do *not* use ordinary toothpaste.

Eyes

The eyes of a healthy dog do not require any special care. The secretion which gathers at the inner corner of the eye may be removed with a piece of cotton wool. If there is any suspicion of an infection, take the dog to the vet.

DOG BREEDING

You may have a bitch which complies with all the prerequisites for breeding a litter. The conditions breed dogs must fulfil vary according to the different breeds; usually they must have attained a certain standing at a show and, in the case of some breeds, must also have passed the required tests in obedience and field trials. Naturally the bitch must be of the required age. An expert from your particular breed club will advise you and help you to select the most suitable mate. Most countries have different rules and regulations concerning dogs and their breeding and it is recommended that you seek Kennel Club or breed society advice as to the conditions you must fulfil.

As a rule a bitch is on heat twice a year – in the spring and again in the autumn. Only during this period is she willing to accept a dog. Even though you may have no breeding experience as yet, you will recognise that the bitch is on heat by the fact that dogs show greater interest in her, that she urinates more frequently, that her vulva is swollen and reddened, and that drops of pink or red fluid fall from the vagina. Generally the bitch is on heat for fourteen to twenty-one days; young bitches for longer, older bitches for a shorter period. The most suitable time to take the bitch to the dog is usually between the ninth and thirteenth day of this period. The exact time depends not only on the age of the bitch but also varies according to the individual. The bitch is always taken to the dog for mating and not the other way round. (In a strange environment a dog is often more interested in his surroundings than in a bitch.) After the dog has mounted the bitch the two remain locked in position for some time because the dog's penis is swollen and can only be withdrawn from the vagina after it has returned to its normal size.

Pregnancy lasts 58–65 days – you can count on an average of 63 days. Twenty days after mating the fertilised eggs become embedded in the lining of the womb and the placentas through which they receive nourishment are formed. During pregnancy the bitch's rate of metabolism increases, as does her requirement of calcium and phosphorus, and her pulse increases to a certain degree. The growth of the developing foetuses changes the shape of the womb, which expands and descends into the lower part of the abdomen. The mammary glands become enlarged and the teats are well visible among the hairs of the bitch's belly.

Whelping box

During pregnancy the bitch must have plenty of exercise, without taxing her strength, and plenty of minerals and vitamins in her diet. About a month before the expected arrival of the puppies you may give the bitch a mild worming cure as the puppies may become infected by parasites while still inside the mother's body. Naturally all must be made ready for the whelping. The bitch usually gives birth in a whelping box. The sides must not be too high, so that the pregnant bitch can enter it easily; nor should they be so low that the puppies can fall out.

As a rule it is not necessary to help the bitch during whelping; she should do everything herself. Bitches of breeds with an undershot bite (e.g. Pekingese, French Bulldog, Bulldog, Boxer, etc.) sometimes have difficulty in freeing a pup from the amniotic sac and biting off the umbilical cord. In such a case you must come to the bitch's aid. Free the pup and cut the umbilical cord with sterilised scissors. Always have your vet's telephone number on hand. If no puppy has emerged within six hours of the beginning of whelping, it means there is some complication that only a vet can attend to. If the contractions cease, dead puppies might be retained within the bitch. Here, too, the vet can come to her aid – usually an injection of the hormone produced by the pituitary gland will start the contractions again.

Sometimes the bitch may get an attack of convulsions several days, or as soon as several hours, after the arrival of the puppies. This is called eclampsia and is caused by a sudden drop in the level of calcium and phosphorus in the blood. In such a case the bitch must be given a calcium injection immediately.

It is important that the puppies begin nursing as soon as they are born. The colostrum secreted from the mammary glands for a few days after the birth contains gammaglobulins which carry all the mother's antigens, thereby giving the pups immunity to infectious diseases.

It may happen that for some reason the mother does not have milk or it dries up, and then you must feed the puppies yourself. Nowadays you can buy suitable substitutes for the mother's milk from your vet. Always consult your vet as to the best method of feeding. Pups fed in this manner must always have their bellies and the area round the anus rubbed with a piece of damp cotton wool after every meal so that they will evacuate their bowels. This is a substitute for the massage the bitch gives them with her tongue.

If the puppies develop normally in the bitch's care they will usually begin taking solid food at the end of the fifth week, but often as early as the third or fourth week. In the sixth week give the puppies oatmeal or rice gruel together with ground or finely minced meat and vegetables. By the seventh week or at the latest the eighth week, the puppies should already be accustomed to solid food and the mother will stop nursing altogether.

In breeds where the standard specifies that the tail be docked it is necessary to ask your vet to do this when the puppies are only two or three days old.

THE SICK DOG

Your days with your dog may not always be happy ones. If there is a change in its behaviour, if it has a temperature, a more rapid pulse, more laboured breathing, diarrhoea or constipation, a discharge from its nose or eyes, if it shows a sign of pain when touched, etc., it is sick. If you suspect your dog is unwell or in pain, the quickest and safest way to help it is to visit the vet.

Very few illnesses can be diagnosed by the dog's owner. These are first and foremost diseases caused by parasites, either external parasites (lice, ticks, fleas), or internal parasites (threadworms, tapeworms), evidence of which may be present in the dog's excrement – either the whole parasites or segments of their bodies. The novice will do best to call in the vet in such cases; the experienced owner will know how to deal with these conditions alone.

Most greatly feared is a virus disease generally known as distemper. This is actually a whole complex of diseases which, three to seven days after infection, are marked by listlessness, loss of appetite, fluctuating temperature, reddening of the mucous membranes and often discharges from the eyes and possibly also the nose. The pulse becomes more rapid, the dog's breathing more laboured, the dog begins coughing. In some dogs there may also be various symptoms of nervous disorders – skin troubles, and the like. Distemper mainly strikes young animals, up to the age of two years. Often it leaves permanent or long-term effects even in animals that have been cured.

Another dangerous illness is infectious inflammation of the liver, called infectious hepatitis. The time of greatest danger to dogs is at the age of two to three months. This disease has no specifically characteristic symptoms, which often resemble those of distemper.

The year 1977–78 saw the appearance of a new virus disease called parvovirus. Clinically its symptoms are primarily frequent vomiting and diarrhoea. Dogs of all ages may be affected by this disease although puppies are, naturally, more greatly endangered.

Effective vaccines are available for all these diseases and you must ask your vet at what age your pups should be vaccinated and, in the case of annual booster vaccinations, when they should be vaccinated again.

Rabies is, of course, one of the most extremely dangerous virus diseases. Thankfully it is not present in the UK although it is to be found in many other parts of the world. It is transmitted through the bite of an infected animal. Rabies is fatal. In most countries of the world vaccination against this disease, fatal also for people, is compulsory.

IMPORTANT TERMINOLOGY

In the text accompanying the pictures in this book you will come across special terms which need to be explained. First of all there are the names given to the various parts of the dog's body. The line drawing shown here will explain this better than a detailed description. It will also show how the height of the dog is measured. Unless stated otherwise height is always measured at the shoulders.

In some breeds it is stressed that pronounced sexual characteristics are demanded by the standard. What is meant by this, of course, is not difference in the sexual organs, but in general outward appearance. A dog is usually more robust, has a heavier, broader and more angular head, more powerful jaws, a thicker neck and his stance is more self-assured. A bitch has a more delicate body structure, a lighter and narrower head, weaker jaws and a more delicate neck. Her stance is usually not as self-assured. These differences are not always distinct, which is why they are mentioned only in the case of certain breeds where they are more striking.

Further terms have to do with colouring. Patches are large markings of solid colour on a lighter background; a saddle is a saddle-shaped dark marking on the back, a mantle is the dark portion of the coat on the shoulders, back and sides. Roan is the name given to a dog with patches and small dark spots or individual dark hairs scattered throughout a pale background. Brindle is definite dark transverse stripes on a lighter background.

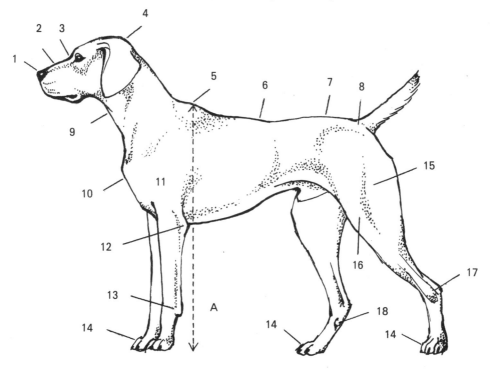

A dog's body: 1, nose; 2, muzzle; 3, stop; 4, occiput or crown; 5, shoulders; 6, back; 7, croup; 8, root of tail; 9, throat; 10, chest; 11, line of shoulder; 12, elbow; 13, pastern joint; 14, toes; 15, thigh; 16, stifle; 17, hock; 18, dewclaws; A, measuring height at the shoulder

Markings: 1, patches; 2, spots; 3, saddle;
4, mantle; 5, brindled

Some colours have unusual names. Sable is brownish-black or brownish-grey, resembling the colour of dark sable fur, isabella is a light straw to yellowish colour, tan is ochre-reddish-brown, apricot or apricosa is as its name implies. Quite unusual is blue merle – a silvery blue splashed and dappled with black, russet-brown and white markings. As it is hard to describe in words it is recommended that you look at the picture of the Collie on page 36.

The colouring of the head may also have certain distinctive aspects and the markings may be given specific names. A dog may have a blaze (a pale mark or band on the forehead); a mask (dark-coloured face); spectacles (a lighter coloured face, mainly the area round the eyes, contrasting with a dark crown), or yellow or red – mahogany – markings placed symmetrically on the lips, cheeks and above the eyes. If there are also similar markings on the inside of the ears, the inner side of the limbs (usually extending to the pastern and hock), the thighs and underneath the tail, and if the dog is coloured black, then the colouring is referred to as black and tan.

26

COLOUR PLATES

WORKING DOGS

Alaskan Malamute

The Siberian Eskimoes gradually settled other Arctic regions of Alaska, Canada and Greenland, taking their dogs with them. In time separate breeds developed in the various regions. A breed of sled-dog that originated in northwestern Alaska was later given the name Malamute, after one of the Eskimo tribes that settled there. Originally these dogs were bred with a single aim – to give peak performance. They were used mainly to pull sleds but also to defend property and for hunting. Only the hardiest specimens could endure the extremely harsh Alaskan winters. When Europeans came to Alaska they, too, began using Malamutes to pull their sleds.

The end of the pioneering days of the conquest of the north brought with it a decline in the breeding of the Alaskan Malamute. Only in recent times, when dog sleds began to be used for sport, did the breed start to make a comeback. Because of its relatively heavy build the Alaskan Malamute is used primarily for long-distance runs requiring endurance, on which it has set many records. It is not as well suited for speed races as other, lighter breeds, but it gives a better performance in pulling heavy loads.

The Alaskan Malamute is friendly, intelligent, obedient, responsive to training and good with children. It requires a firm hand, however, especially when the dogs are kept and driven in a pack, for then there is a constant struggle for social superiority among the pack.

Height: dog 64–71 cm, bitch 58–66 cm, preferably the upper limit in both instances. **Weight:** 38–56 kg. **Colour:** all shades from light grey to black with a white mask and white underparts, the mantle and top of the head being darker than the rest of the body (1). Of the single solid colours only white is allowed. Spotting or irregular marks are undesirable. The tail is carried high but must not be curled over the back. The Alaskan Malamute differs from the similar Siberian Husky by having a more massive build, shorter body, heavier, broader head and the muzzle less narrowed toward the end. Besides the more common harnessing of dogs one behind the other in a line, Alaskan Malamutes are often harnessed in a fan-like arrangement, suitable primarily for travel on flat plains (2).

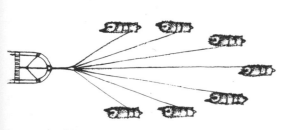

2

1

The Boxer's elegant present-day appearance is a relatively recent development. The breed's roots go back as far as the Middle Ages, to Bavaria where the Danziger Bullenbeiszer, Brabanter Bullenbeiszer, Mastiff and English Bulldog were crossed to obtain dogs that could be used for hunting heavy game as well as for the dog fights which were very popular at the time. Up until 1890 the Boxer was much larger and heavier than now and looked more like a Mastiff. The Klub der deutschen Boxer-Freunde (Boxer Friends Club), founded in Germany in 1896, deserves credit for the strict selective breeding that gave the Boxer its present-day harmonious build and outstanding character traits. The year 1904 is the date of the first standard, and as of 1926 the Boxer was officially classed in the international service dog group. The present standard places great emphasis on the dog's overall harmonious appearance — the various parts of the body must all be mutually in the required proportions. The important feature on the head is the proportion of the muzzle to the crown. The muzzle must not be too short; the closer its breadth comes to that of the crown the better.

The Boxer is intelligent, calm and docile and at the same time an excellent watchdog. It is a good companion and is fond of children. It retains its character well into advanced age, a time when dogs of other breeds tend to be glum and grumpy. Its short, close-lying, glossy coat does not require any special care and this, too, contributes to its popularity as a housedog.

2 ♂

Height: dog 57–63 cm, bitch 53–59 cm. **Weight:** dog 30–32 kg, bitch 25–27 kg. **Colour:** fawn or brindle (1), the fawn in shades from dark deer-red to pale fawn. Deer-red (2) is considered the most handsome colour. There is a dark mask on the face. The brindle Boxer should have dark to black stripes, which must not merge, on a fawn ground (in the aforesaid shades). White markings are permitted as long as they are not an indication of insufficient pigmentation, i.e. they must not exceed one-third of the body area, the head must not be white, there must not be any pink markings, etc.

The ears are cropped to a point (3) in some European countries. In Britain, however, cropping is not permitted and the ears retain their original shape (4).

3

4

1 ♂

Briard (Berger de Brie), Beauceron and Cane da Pastore Bergamasco

The name of this shepherd dog does not originate from the region of Brie, noted for its cheese, but is probably a corrupted version of 'Chien d'Aubry'. In 1317 a dog of this breed is said to have traced the murderer of his master, a nobleman by the name of Aubry de Montdidier. Because of its handsome appearance and docile disposition the Briard became probably the most popular of the French breeds.

The Beauceron or Berger de Beauce is probably descended from the same ancestors as the Briard. Previously it was considered to be merely a short-haired variety of the Briard. It is interesting to note that in this instance also the dog's name has no connection with its place of origin, which is not the region of Beauce but of Brie. The Beauceron is an excellent breed of shepherd dog, intelligent, obedient, and often used for police work. These dogs are quite excitable and sometimes unpredictable, however, and thus are not at all suitable as companions for children.

In the mountains of northern Italy one will find interesting sheepdogs whose appearance indicates that they are related to the Briard. The breed is called Cane da Pastore Bergamasco, or sometimes Bergamaschi. According to dog breeding authorities, these dogs carry a strain of Persian sheepdog blood and perhaps also of Hungarian dog blood. The Bergamasco is a courageous, reliable watchdog, but because of its shaggy coat it is not particularly situable as a housedog.

2 ♂

Briard (1)
Height: dog 62–68 cm, bitch 56–64 cm.
Weight: not prescribed. **Colour:** all solid colours except white are permitted. Darker shades are preferred.

Beauceron
Height: dog 60–70 cm, bitch 58–68 cm. **Weight:** 27–37 kg. **Colour:** black, black and tan (2), pale red with black-tipped primary hairs, grey, grey with black markings.

Dewclaws are given as a typical characteristic by the standard but the FCI leaves it up to the individual memeber countries whether to permit their removal or not.

Cane da Pastore Bergamasco (3)
Height: 55–63 cm. **Weight:** about 30 kg.
Colour: any shade of grey with white or
black markings or without markings, but
a black saddle is not allowed. Also
permitted are white, isabella and fawn.

1

33

This breed originated in England in the late eighteenth century, by crossing the Mastiff with the Bulldog. Originally these dogs were used by gamekeepers for protection against poachers on their nightly rounds. The Bullmastiff's outstanding qualities also began to be used later by other defenders of the law and in 1924 the National Bullmastiff Police Club published the first standard for this breed.

Although the Bullmastiff's body is massive, it still has an elegant appearance, radiating strength and calm. It has a broad, angular head, powerful jaws and a muzzle which should be no longer than 8–9 cm. The forehead, unlike that of the Mastiff, is flat and it has a slightly marked stop. The relatively small V-shaped ears may be pressed close to the head or may stick out slightly in the form of a half-shell.

A well-trained Bullmastiff is a dangerous adversary. In substance, however, it is kind, happy, trustworthy, faithful, courageous and very obedient. Another of its great merits is its excellent relationship with children. It is more lively than the Mastiff and more manageable. The Bullmastiff is very hardy and its short, smooth, dense coat does not require any special attention, merely brushing, first with a medium-hard and then with a soft brush to remove all grime, followed by smoothing with a chamois leather or flannel cloth to give the coat the desired sheen.

Height: dog 63.5–68.5 cm, bitch 61–66 cm. **Weight:** dog 49.9–59 kg, bitch 41–49.9 kg. **Colour:** permitted by the standard is any shade of fawn, red or brindle (1). The ears, nose and muzzle should be black. Dogs with a dark mask are preferred. The eyes should be dark brown or hazel, the eyelids must be dark, and the folds of skin between the eyes should be dark (2).

At first glance the Bullmastiff might easily be confused with the Mastiff. The following points should be noted: the Bullmastiff has less wrinkled skin on the head and face, the muzzle is longer, and the lips are not as pendulous, the body outline is shorter than the Mastiff's, the tail is set higher up, and the ears are set higher up as well.

2

1 ♀

Collie

The Collie, one of the handsomest breeds of shepherd dogs, originated in the harsh climate of Scotland. The name is derived from a breed of sheep kept in Scotland in the eighteenth century. These sheep, with black face and black legs, were called colley sheep and the dogs that guarded and watched over the grazing flocks became known as colley-dogs. The first pictures of these dogs, which did not have the long handsome coat of present-day Collies, date from the year 1790. Colley-dogs were crossed with Irish Setters and with Borzois, from which they inherited certain features of the skull and the narrow chest, as well as their manner of movement, thereby gradually giving rise to Collies as we know them today.

As late as the early nineteenth century the Collie was a relatively unknown breed and it was not until it appeared at its first shows that it began to gain in favour. Fashion raised this breed to the pinnacle of popularity a number of times and to this day the Collie continues to be one of the most popular breeds.

The Collie is an intelligent, trainable and faithful dog of elegant, dignified appearance and because of these qualities it is in great demand as a pet. It is reserved with strangers, has an innate talent for herding and guarding sheep, and its dense, long coat provides good protection in bad weather. Besides the familiar long-haired Rough Collie with a full coat (1), also kept, but far less commonly, is the short-haired Smooth Collie with a harsh and smooth coat lying close to the body (3).

2

Height: dog 56–61 cm, bitch 51–56 cm. **Weight:** dog 20.5–29.5 kg, bitch 18–25 kg. Collies are divided, according to the colour of their coats, into sable and white, tricolour and blue merle. Examples of the first are sable without markings except white. The commonest colouring is golden-yellow with a white mane and white markings on the legs (1). Tricoloured Collies are black and tan with white markings. Blue merle Collies (2) are silvery blue with black markings and, preferably, tan markings, although these may be absent. The standard allows any colours and markings but in judging preference is given to dogs with handsome markings.

3 ♂

Whatever the dog's colour it must
always have a black nose. The eyes
should be almond-shaped and dark
brown. The one exception is if the coat
is blue merle, in which case the eyes
may be blue or blue-flecked.

Bearded Collie: see p. 67.

1

This breed is named after Friedrich L. Dobermann, night watchman and tax collector, who lived in Apolda (Thüringen) in 1834–94. Requiring a dog for his protection and finding none that was suitable for the purpose, he bred his own, very sharp breed from dogs that he bought at the market or caught as strays. After he died Otto Göller (or Göllner according to some sources) took over, adding the blood of shepherd dogs, pointers, Rottweilers, greyhounds and Manchester Terriers, and also improving the breed's character. It was not long before the police became interested in the Dobermann because it had many traits that were eminently suitable for police work. It is faithful, courageous, alert and has an excellent nose. It is suspicious of strangers and defends its owner ruthlessly. Naturally a dog with such traits requires a firm hand during training and it is definitely not a dog for everybody.

In both world wars the Dobermann proved its worth in the medical corps, intelligence service and as a guard dog, primarily in the tropics because it stands up well to high temperatures. Another welcome feature is that its short, hard, dense, close-lying coat does not need any special attention. Nowadays the Dobermann is mostly used as a service dog or watchdog.

Height: dog 69 cm, bitch 65 cm.
Weight: not officially prescribed.
Colour: black (1), dark brown (2), fawn or blue (3), with rusty-red, sharply defined markings on the muzzle, lips, cheeks, upper eyelids, throat, pastern and feet, inner thighs, anus and two on the chest. The Dobermann's ears are set high (4). They are not cropped in the UK.
Dogue de Bordeaux: see p. 90

3 ♂   2 ♂

4

1 ♀

German Shepherd Dog (Alsatian)

The German Shepherd Dog traces its origin to the dogs that were used in Germany as shepherd dogs, both herding and protecting flocks of sheep from wolves. In the 1800s they began to be selectively bred by some breeders, and 22 April 1899 saw the founding of the Verein für deutsche Schäferhunde (German Shepherd Dog Society) in Stuttgart. Breeding focused mainly on performance and was not restricted merely to improvement of the dog's external appearance. The German Shepherd Dog thus became a truly versatile dog. Nowadays it is used as a watchdog, police dog, tracker, by the health service, as an avalanche rescue dog and as one of the most widely used guide-dogs for the blind. It is very adaptable, responsive to training and lively, but basically may be characterised as faithful to a single owner or a one-man dog.

Generally the German Shepherd's coat is of hard, dense, close-lying hair (1). However some German Shepherds have a long, hard coat with hairs that are not quite straight and do not lie close to the body (2). Inside and behind the ears, on the back of the forearms and in the region of the shoulders the coat is much longer than elsewhere on the body. The long, hard coat is not as resistant to weather as the short, dense coat, but if the undercoat is sufficiently dense the dog is good for breeding.

A third type is a dog with long hair but generally without the undercoat and with the hair on the back divided by a parting. Sometimes such dogs are called Altdeutscher Schäferhund. They are not allowed to be used for breeding.

2 ♀

Height: dog 62–66 cm, bitch 51–55 cm. (2–5 cm above or below these heights is permissible.) **Weight:** not prescribed. The proportion of height to body length should be 9:10 (the body should have a rectangular outline), the sexual characteristic must be clearly evident. **Colour:** black, steel grey, ash grey, so-called wolf colour, reddish-yellow or reddish-brown, either a solid colour or with regular brown, yellow to whitish-grey patches, also with a black saddle. In black dogs the undercoat is black, in others it is slightly lighter than the primary hairs. Small white patches on the chest are permitted. The definite colouring of the puppies may be determined only after they have acquired the primary hairs.

3

The hind legs sometimes bear a fifth, vestigial digit called a dewclaw (3). Because this is often torn when the dog is older, it should be removed shortly after birth.

1 ♂

Great Dane

Dogs like the Great Dane are a lighter type of Mastiff used for hunting. In the late sixteenth and the seventeenth centuries Mastiffs were often crossed with large Irish Wolfhounds and their hybrid offspring were very popular at the courts of German princes, where they were used to hunt large game. They wore padded or iron armour and spiked collars. The largest and best dogs were used for selective breeding which eventually produced dogs roughly like the present-day Great Dane. Commonest were two types – a lighter type called Ulmer Dogge and a heavier type called Danziger Dogge, later Dänische Dogge (Danish Dog), although it had no connection with Denmark. The name stuck, however, and in English was translated as Great Dane. As early as 1876, at an exhibition in Hamburg, it was suggested that the breed should be made uniform and three years later this was put into effect. Breeders launched a planned programme to obtain strong, large dogs which were courageous and possessed steadfast endurance. Few other breeds have been developed with such love, diligence and perseverance as the Great Dane, often called the Apollo of dogs.

The Great Dane is an intelligent and trustworthy dog but suspicious of strangers. It can be a dangerous opponent, which will attack quickly and without a sound. Dogs of this type have relatively poor hearing and it is recommended that you keep talking to it when approaching such a dog, particularly at night. Training is not easy because the Great Dane does not tolerate coercive methods.

Height: dog 76–90 cm, bitch at least 71 cm. **Weight:** dog 54 kg, bitch 46 kg. **Colour:** may be of five different kinds: brindle (3), ground colour pale buff to rich gold with definite black transverse stripes; fawn (1), with a black mask; blue, light grey to pure steel blue (paler eyes are permitted); black, glossy black with the darkest possible eyes and black nails; and finally harlequin, with the ground colour pure white with

4

symmetrically placed glossy black or blue markings (2). Also belonging to this group is the type of coloration called Manteltiger, where the black forms a mantle and only the neck, legs and tip of the tail are pure white. The ears are set high on the head (4). They are not cropped in the UK.

2 ♀   3 ♂

1

Groenendael and Tervueren

The Groenendael breed of shepherd dog was named after Groenendael Castle located south of Brussels. The selective breeding of indigenous dogs at the turn of the century, by crossing closely related individuals, produced slender, long-legged dogs with a long, dense, smooth coat, which were intelligent and versatile. When training these dogs, however, it must be remembered that Groenendaels are very sensitive and do not tolerate harsh methods.

The Tervueren is a very similar breed differing only in colour. Its origin dates from the year 1895 and the breed is considered to have been created by the Belgian breeder F. Corbeel. Groenendael blood also figured in the initial stages of breeding. The greatest credit for the breeding of Tervuerens probably goes to a farmer named Tuykom, who is said to have prided himself on having the largest beets, the handsomest cabbages and the best dogs. His methods, however, were very harsh. Any bitch that did not fit his concept of the ideal was killed. The characteristics of the Tervueren are the same as those of the Groenendael.

Until recently all breeds of Belgian shepherd dogs were confined in distribution to their country of origin. However, when the Groenendael won the European Guard and Utility Dog Championship twice in a row a few years ago the breed began to gain in popularity and is now appearing with increasing frequency at training grounds as well as shows.

Groenendael (1)
Height: dog 61–66 cm, bitch 56–61 cm.
Weight: 28–35 kg. **Colour:** black, or black with limited white patches on chest and feet.

Tervueren (2)
Height and weight: the same as those of the Groenendael but the colour is not black. The coat should be reddish-fawn with the tip of each hair black, thus giving it a sable sheen. Dogs with a dark mask are preferred.

3

4

To the layman both breeds may appear
to resemble a small German Shepherd
Dog at first glance. The latter, however,
has a rectangular body outline whereas
Belgian shepherd dogs are squarer. Also
typical are the differences in the
characteristics of the head. The skulls of
Belgian shepherd dogs are flatter and
the muzzles are longer than the
braincases (4). The skull of the German
Shepherd Dog is more arched, with the
muzzle being the same length as the
braincase (3). The German Shepherd
Dog has slightly slanting,
almond-shaped eyes. The eyes of
Belgian shepherd dogs must not be
slanting.

2

1

Hovawart

This is probably a very old breed of which written mention is made as far back as the thirteenth century. At that time such dogs guarded herds as well as farmyards. The name Hovawart, apparently derived from the German words *Hof* (farm) and *warte* (stay), was also used at that time. These dogs occurred most often in the Harz mountain district. Gradually, however, they began to disappear. Not until the turn of the nineteenth and twentieth centuries did breeders in the Harz, Black Forest and central German highlands begin to regenerate, or recreate, this breed from the long-haired dogs with shaggy tail and drop ears kept by the peasants of these regions. From the very start the breeders proceeded very systematically – every dog was tattooed and records were kept. The external appearance soon became fixed and in 1936 the breed received official recognition.

At first Hovawarts appeared only very occasionally at shows, but their popularity is continually growing, not only in Germany but elsewhere as well, and primarily in Switzerland, Italy and the Netherlands. The Hovawart is a calm, well-balanced dog which has many uses. It is good-natured and good with children, fierce when defending its owner or its owner's property, but manageable. Nowadays it is used as a faithful and trustworthy guard and police dog. The Hovawart's coat is long and slightly wavy but, apart from daily brushing and occasional combing, it requires no other special care.

2 3

Height: dog 63–70 cm, bitch 58–65 cm.
Weight: dog 30–40 kg, bitch 25–35 kg.
Colour: the colouring is divided into three groups. Black with gold markings (1), black ground colour with golden-yellow to golden-brown markings which, on the head, run parallel to the bridge of the muzzle to a point under the eyes and down onto the throat. There are distinct spots above the eyes. The mark on the breast should not extend onto the forelegs; on the latter the marking extends in front from the toes to the pastern joint, and at the back up to the body. On the hind legs the marking should extend practically to the belly but viewed from the side only a narrow band up the front of the legs should be visible. The marking beneath

the root of the tail must be distinct.
A white spot on the breast no larger
than 6 cm and single white hairs at the
tip of the tail are allowed. Black (2) —
deep black without any white hairs.
Blond (3) – a uniform golden-yellow
throughout. In both black and blond
a small white spot on the breast and/or
single white hairs at the tip of the tail
are permissible.

1

Leonberg, near the city of Stuttgart, was the home of Heinrich Essig, town councillor and great animal lover, during the years 1808–89. Yearly he raised and sold about 300 dogs, and he also kept poultry and various game animals. In 1846 he began developing a new breed of dogs by crossing the Landseer, the long-haired Saint Bernard and the Pyrenean Mountain Dog. At first the offspring were very heterogeneous and it was not until the Internationale Leonberger Club, founded in Stuttgart in 1895, and in later years other Leonberger clubs furthered its development that the breed acquired uniform characteristics, allowing a standard to be formulated in 1901. The standard corresponds to Essig's endeavour to develop a lion-like dog resembling the emblem of his native town. The Leonberger has a calm disposition, is docile and is fond of children. It is very active considering its size.

If you travel in Turkey you might encounter large dogs resembling the Leonberger in build and colouring but short-haired and longer in the body. These are representatives of a very ancient breed of Anatolian Shepherd Dogs called the Karabash. They are possibly descended from the Mastiffs that existed in the Middle East as far back as 3,000 years ago. They are wary, intrepid watchdogs. They arrived in Europe only recently; the first were brought to England in 1965.

2 ♂

Leonberger
Height: dog 72–80 cm, bitch 65–75 cm. **Weight:** 60–80 kg. **Colour:** lion-colour (1), golden-yellow or rusty-yellow with a dark mask. Dark- to black-tipped hairs are allowed; in exceptional instances the absence of the dark mask is also allowed. The collar and underside of the tail and trousers as well as the feathering on the front legs may be slightly paler but must not disrupt the harmony of the general colouring. The coat is medium long and lies close to the body, and there is a well-developed mane on the neck and chest.

Karabash (2)
Height: dog 74–81 cm, bitch 71–79 cm.
Weight: dog 50–64 kg, bitch 41–59 kg.
Colour: cream to golden brown with
a dark mask and dark ears. The coat is
short and dense. In Turkey the ears are
cropped, in Europe the natural
V-shaped drop ears are retained.

1 ♀

The Mastiff is a very old breed; in Europe it is definitely one of the oldest. Originally these dogs were used in battle but in medieval days they began to be used also for hunting bears, wolves and boars. The Mastiff holds the dog record for size and weight because some individuals weigh over 100 kg. The originally non-uniform breed of relatively different types of Mastiffs was made uniform round 1835 and as of 1883 was governed by the standard which is valid to this day. Basically the Mastiff is good-natured and friendly but only towards people it knows well. Towards strangers it is aggressive and, when irritated, may be quite dangerous.

Spain is the home of the closely related Mastin Español or Spanish Mastiff. The dogs bred in Estremadura province are a lighter and more lively type, those bred in Leon province are heavier and calmer. It is a good-natured dog and gentle towards people, particularly children, but towards other dogs and larger mammals it is unfriendly and aggressive. This characteristic was bred into the breed in the days when it defended flocks of sheep against wolves.

In their conquest of America the Spaniards brought with them various Mastiff-type dogs. Later crossings with indigenous dogs produced various breeds, e.g. in Brazil the Fila Brasileiro, a breed used to defend farms, drive cattle, and track game. Their character is similar to that of the Mastiff.

2 ♂

Mastiff
Height: at least 75 cm. **Weight:** 75–90 kg, sometimes more. **Colour** allowed by the standard: various shades of fawn (1), silver, apricot and brindle. The mask and ears are almost black, the nose always black. The muscles of the temples are well developed, the jaw muscles are extremely strong.

Mastin Español
Height: dog 65–71 cm, bitch about 67 cm. **Weight:** 50–60 kg. **Colour:** golden-yellow, reddish (2), white with patches or with golden-yellow or red markings. The skin is pale pink. The coat is always darker at the base than at the tips and is longer than the Mastiff's. The nose must be black. The loose skin on the neck forms two folds on the underside of the neck.

Fila Brasileiro (3)
Height: more than 68 cm. **Weight:** about 60 kg. **Colour:** all solid colours or brindle are permitted, except white, which may be only on the feet and tip of the tail.

3 ♂

1 ♀

Neapolitan Mastiff and Tibetan Mastiff

Fighting dogs accompanied warrior kings' armies in the most ancient times. Later strong fighting dogs also accompanied the Roman legions. The Roman Molossus Dogs and Epiran fighting dogs were the most famous. When the Romans invaded the British Isles, however, they discovered dogs which outclassed their fighting dogs in size as well as ferociousness. Some of these dogs were later taken home by the Romans and crossed with fighting dogs. The hybrid offspring were used initially in battle and later also in the arena, in combat with wild beasts and gladiators. These dogs are the ancestors of the breed called the Neapolitan Mastiff.

Opinions as to the character of this breed vary. Some breeders say they are calm, faithful, obedient, and good watchdogs which attack only on command, others that they are difficult to control and may even be dangerous to their owners. The truth of the matter is that the Neopolitan Mastiff is a self-confident dog that is not readily dominated. However, in the correct hands it is a very fine dog.

The origin of all breeds of Mastiff-type dogs must be sought in the centre of Asia. Generally they are considered to be descended from the Tibetan Mastiff. This large, long-haired, centuries-old breed is used to this day for herding yaks and guarding the houses and tents of Asia's mountain inhabitants. They are obedient dogs and responsive to training, but distrustful, excitable and unfriendly towards strangers.

2 ♂

Neapolitan Mastiff
Height: dog 65–75 cm, bitch 60–70 cm.
Weight: 50–70 kg. **Colour:** black (1), lead-grey, brindle or brown. White markings on the breast and toes are allowed.

Tibetan Mastiff
Height: dog 66 cm, bitch 61 cm. **Weight:** about 75 kg. **Colour:** black with red or yellow markings (2) or wheaten with black and white markings that must not exceed one-quarter of the overall colour and must be confined to the legs, feet and chest.

The dogs of both breeds have small drop ears. In Europe those of the Neapolitan Mastiff are often cropped to the so-called *kampf-schnitt* form, leaving only the very base of the cartilaginus lobe of the outer ear (3). That is how the ears of fighting dogs were cropped in bygone days in order that their adversary could not seize them by the sensitive ear lobe.

3

1

Newfoundland and Landseer

In the late nineteenth century large shaggy dogs were brought to Europe from Newfoundland by British and French sailors. In their native land these dogs had been used mainly for helping fishermen by dragging nets and drawing carts and sleighs. Their great strength, hardiness – weather-wise and work-wise – as well as extraordinary skill in swimming predetermined them for this work. Purposeful breeding strengthened the dogs' unusual natural talent for retrieving objects from water, and that is why Newfoundlands have often been used to rescue drowning people. The Newfoundland is very lively and temperamental considering its size, intelligent and self-confident but very likeable. Its long-haired coat, which often becomes matted behind the ears, on the neck and round the genitalia, is relatively demanding to care for. It must be combed daily and brushed frequently, taking care not to disrupt the structure of the undercoat unduly (do not comb right down to the skin). Working in water often causes ear infections and for that reason it is necessary to pay particular attention to cleaning the dog's ears.

Until the year 1959 self-coloured and black and white dogs were considered to be merely colour races of the same breed and were exhibited together as such. Following numerous debates, however, the FCI suggested the two be separated and in 1960 laid down the standard for each separate breed. Black dogs retained the original name and the slightly larger black and white dogs were named after the English painter Sir Edwin Landseer, by whom they were often painted.

2

Newfoundland (1)
Height: dog 71 cm, bitch 66 cm. **Weight:** dog 64–69 kg, bitch 50–54.5 kg. **Colour:** deep coal black; a slight tinge of bronze on the breast and toes is acceptable. Formerly there were also bronze-coloured specimens but these are practically never seen nowadays. The coat is thick and coarse and lies close to the body.

Landseer (2)
Height: dog 72–80 cm, bitch 67–72 cm.
Weight: dog 55–60 kg, bitch 50–55 kg.
Colour: clear white with individual black patches on the body and loins. The neck, chest, belly, legs and tail must be white. The head is black; ideally there should be white on the muzzle extending backwards from the nose to form a narrow, symmetrical blaze. The coat, except on the head, should be long, as smooth as possible, fine textured, and not as thick as the Newfoundland's.

Old English Sheepdog, South Russian Owtcharka and Cumberland Sheepdog

The Old English Sheepdog is one of the oldest breeds of shepherd dogs but its origin is obscure. According to some authorities its ancestry includes the South Russian Owtcharka and perhaps also the French Briard. It is a medium-sized dog but its abundant, shaggy coat makes it look very roubst. The puppies are born with a rudimentary tail, but it is usually completely docked at the base. The Old English Sheepdog has a typical voice – its bark sounds like someone beating on a cracked pot. It is a calm, intelligent dog, wary but not timid, and very fond of children.

The South Russian Owtcharka, whose blood figures in that of the Old English Sheepdog, nowadays occurs from the Crimea to the southern Ukraine, but its origin must be sought in Asturias in northern Spain, whence came the dogs that accompanied flocks of Merino sheep imported into Russia. These were crossed with Tartar dogs, giving rise to the South Russian Owtcharka breed, dogs which are responsive to training and which make reliable shepherd dogs. They were given official recognition as an independent breed at the International Cynological Congress in 1952.

The Old English Sheepdog could readily be confused with the Cumberland Sheepdog. The latter, however, is bigger, hairier, and usually has a long, shaggy tail.

Old English Sheepdog
Height: dog at least 61 cm, bitch at least 56 cm. **Weight:** 25–30 kg. **Colour:** may be all shades of grey, grizzle, blue-grey (1) or blue merle, with or without white markings.

South Russian Owtcharka
Height: 62–65 cm. **Weight:** 35–40 kg. Dogs must be distinctly different from bitches. **Colour:** may be white (2), white tinged with yellow, ash-grey with small or large spots, or white with a grey undercoat which gives a bluish impression.

1

Cumberland Sheepdog
Height: over 60 cm. **Weight:** about
35–40 kg. **Colour:** black with a white
blaze, a white spot on the chest, white
feet and a white-tipped tail.

The long, dense coat of all these
breeds has a marked tendency to
become matted, particularly behind the
ears, on the neck, the thighs and round
the anus, and therefore needs to be
combed at least once a day.

Portuguese Shepherd dog: see p. 90.

Pumi, Puli and Komondor

In the ninth century, when the Magyars coming from the east began to settle in Europe, they brought with them their herds and herding dogs which were excellently adapted to the climate of the steppes. Over the years these dogs were developed into three separate breeds of different sizes. In the seventeenth and eighteenth centuries, crossings with the Pomeranian Sheperd's Spitz and the Briard gave rise to the Pumi, a versatile dog used as a shepherd dog and watchdog as well as to kill vermin. The other two breeds are characterised by a unique coat which consists of hair that forms corded tassels. The smallest of the three breeds is the Puli, a typical shepherd dog also used to herd pigs. Apparently the oldest breed is also the largest – the Komondor – used primarily to guard and defend herds.

None of these three breeds makes a good housedog. They are very noisy, temperamental and often aggressive, and their coats require considerable attention. The Pumi is the simplest to care for as its shaggy coat does not become matted and needs brushing only once a week. Puli and Komondor puppies have a soft fluffy coat which becomes corded only later; in the case of the Komondor not until the ninth month. The corded areas must be divided into tassels or strands roughly the thickness of a pencil, using a special knife or razor blade and working from the base of the coat outwards. Grime and pulled-out hairs must be removed by brushing and the coat checked regularly to see that the separate strands do not become matted.

Bitches of these breeds sometimes partially shed their hair after whelping, primarily on the limbs, belly and chest, and very occasionally over the entire body. Such hair loss may also occur in sick or poorly nourished dogs.

3

Pumi (1)
Height: dog 51 cm, bitch 40.5 cm.
Weight: 8–13 kg. **Colour:** all shades of grey and black.

Puli (2)
Height: dog 40–44 cm, bitch 37–41 cm.
Weight: dog 13–15 kg, bitch 10–13 kg.
Colour: black or black with a rufous tinge, all shades of grey, apricot and white.

2

Komondor (3)

Height: dog about 80 cm but not less than 65 cm, bitch about 70 cm but not less than 55 cm. **Weight:** dog 50–61 kg, bitch 35–50 kg. **Colour:** white.

The skin of all three breeds must be a strongly pigmented slate grey. The nose, gums and nails must also be dark grey or preferably black. Hair combed over the face emphasises the required rounded shape of the head, which, according to the standard, should resemble a ball of hair rising above the line of the back.

1

Pyrenean Mastiff,
Pyrenean Mountain Dog and Kuvasz

The Pyrenean Mastiff belongs to the group of so-called Hungarian breeds whose origin must be sought amongst the dogs brought to Europe either by the Magyars in the ninth century or later by the Kuman tribes in the thirteenth century. The Pyrenean Mastiff occurs on the Spanish as well as the French side of the Pyrenees and both countries contribute to the preservation and further development of the breed. The Spanish and French standard differs, however, although merely in minor aspects. At shows this breed is often combined with the very similar Pyrenean Mountain Dog and the two are probably often mated.

The Pyrenean Mountain Dog originated mainly in the mountain valleys of the Ariège and in Andorra, where it was used to guard flocks against wolves and bears.

In Hungary one will find many breeds whose origin is the same as that of these two breeds. One of the commonest is the Kuvasz, originally also used to guard flocks but also used for hunting wolves and wild boar.

All three breeds are intelligent, courageous and good watchdogs which get along exceedingly well with children. Their handsome coats require attention. Daily brushing and combing are a must because the hair behind the ears, round the anus and round the genitals readily becomes matted.

2

Pyrenean Mastiff
Height: dog 70–81 cm, bitch 65–73.5 cm.
Weight: 45–55 kg. **Colour:** white or white with badger-coloured, pale yellow or wolf-grey patches on the head, ears and at the root of the tail (1). A few patches on the body are allowed. The coat is thick, straight and moderately long, with a fine woolly undercoat.

Pyrenean Mountain Dog (2)
Height: dog 70–81 cm, bitch 65–73.5 cm.
Weight: 45–55 kg. **Colour:** as for the preceding breed; in dogs with patches, badger-coloured patches are preferred. The coat is thick, long, soft, rather fine and slightly wavy at the rear end of the body.

Kuvasz (3)
Height: dog 71–76 cm, bitch 66–71 cm.
Weight: 40–60 cm. **Colour:** white or
ivory. The grey skin must be strongly
pigmented, the nose slate-grey, and the
roof of the mouth black or with black
spots. The coat is rather coarse and
slightly wavy. The coats of puppies are
glossy, thick, smooth or wavy.

3

Rottweiler

This breed takes its name from the town of Rottweil in West Germany. This old Roman settlement grew into a town which was a meeting-place for cattle dealers as far back as the thirteenth century. Rottweilers were used to drive herds of cattle and also to guard the property of merchants and butchers, who would put the day's takings in a purse attached to the dog's collar when they went to the tavern in the evening for a drink. Gradual changes in the organisation of cattle dealing, above all the cessation of cattle droving, resulted in a decrease in the number of these dogs, which were later used only by butchers to pull small carts. Around 1900 it seemed that the breed might become extinct, but at that time wider use began to be made of dogs in police work and, as luck would have it, Rottweilers were among those chosen for this purpose. The breed became extremely popular, especially with the Hamburg police, and its outstanding qualities were rediscovered.

The Rottweiler is calm and good-natured and enjoys working. It is a willing retriever and usually follows tracks eagerly. Considering its weight it is surprisingly agile. It has a firm, hard bite and its attacks are quick and without warning.

Whether driving herds of cattle, searching for and bringing back strays, or doing police work, the dogs have always had to be able to work independently. Weak handling makes these dogs difficult to control because they will try to gain the upper hand (dominant position) in the person-dog relationship. (This, of course, applies not only to Rottweilers but to many other breeds of watchdogs as well.)

Height: dog 63–69 cm, bitch 58–63.5 cm. **Weight:** about 35 kg. **Colour:** black and tan, i.e. with mahogany markings on the cheeks, muzzle, above the eyes, on the legs, and on the chest (1). The nose and lips must be black, the eyes a very dark brown. The skin on the head must fit closely all over and must not form furrows on the forehead. The short tail should stand straight out and should not be set low. It should be docked short. Occasionally a puppy is born with a rudimentary tail, but usually the tail is longer than desirable and must be docked. The proportions of the head are important: the bridge of the muzzle, from the base to the tip of the nose, must not be longer than the skull from the occipital bone to the stop (2).

2

1 ♂

The history of the Saint Bernard is closely linked with the monastery at the Great Saint Bernard Pass in the Alps. Here, too, one will find what is probably the first depiction of the breed, although looking a bit different, in a painting by an unknown artist, dated 1695. The monastery kept huge watchdogs which the monks often used in tracking and saving lost travellers, exhausted and freezing in fierce mountain blizzards. The most famous dog of all was named Barry, who saved the lives of 40 people during his twelve years as a rescue dog. Preserved, stuffed and mounted, after his death, he may be seen to this day by visitors to the natural history museum in Berne. During the monastery's 250-year history some 2,000 people were rescued by these dogs or with their aid. The legendary keg of brandy, however, which in most people's mind is inseparably linked with the image of the Saint Bernard, is a fabrication and no mention of it may be found in the monastery chronicles.

The Saint Bernard is very quiet and friendly, devoted to its owner and family and is especially fond of children. It is wary of strangers. These characteristics make it an excellent watchdog, trustworthy companion and defender of the family. In former times it was often used to pull loads. It has an extremely keen sense of smell and a well-trained Saint Bernard is said to be able to pick up a person's scent in the snowy expanse of the mountains at a distance of three kilometres.

2 ♂

Height: the taller the better, dog at least 75 cm, bitch 70 cm. **Weight:** dog 80–85 kg, bitch 75–78 kg. Bitches are not only smaller and lighter but also have a more subtle build. **Colour:** red and white; the colours must be pure and intense. The bridge of the muzzle, blaze, collar, breast, forelegs, belly, hind legs at least to the hock joint, and the tip of the tail should be white. There may be a red mark, a so-called star, in the white area on the forehead. The red colour may form a mantle (3) extending from the shoulders to the loins and thighs, or patches (4) clearly defined on the white ground.

Originally the Saint Bernard's coat was smooth and short-haired (2). It remained thus until 1830, when the breed was crossed with the Newfoundland, resulting in the long-haired Saint Bernard (1). Today long-haired Saint Bernards are much more common and more popular than the short-haired ones.

3 ♂

4 ♂

1

Shetland Sheepdog (Sheltie) and Bearded Collie

The Shetland Isles, off the north coast of Scotland, have a typical fauna as well as typical domestic animals. You will find here small breeds of sheep as well as small ponies – Shetland ponies. The shepherd dogs which guard the flocks of sheep are likewise small. The Shetland Sheepdog, or Sheltie, sometimes also called a miniature Collie, developed in the islands long ago from crosses between Collies from the British mainland and Icelandic dogs (Islandsk Hund, also called Yakki) brought to the islands by whaling ships. Shelties guarded houses, herded flocks of sheep and ponies, and kept cattle away from fields which were not hedged. As of 1909 the original Shetland Sheepdogs were gradually bred to a uniform standard; breeders in Lerwick founded the Shetland Collie Club and the breed was given official recognition in 1914. Nowadays Shelties are more frequently kept as companion dogs than herding dogs. They are gentle, intelligent, affectionate dogs but are not friendly with everybody. They are good watchdogs but their lively temperament demands plenty of exercise. The long coat with its dense, soft undercoat needs frequent combing and daily brushing.

According to historical records from the year 1514, three Polish Lowland Shepherd Dogs (Owczarek Nizinny), namely a dog and two bitches, were brought to Scotland in exchange for a pair of sheep. These dogs were the ancestors of the Bearded Collie and the Sheltie also carries a strain of their blood.

3

2

Shetland Sheepdog
Height: ideal for a dog is 37 cm and for a bitch 35.5 cm; but a height of 32–38 cm is permitted. **Weight:** 10–18 kg. The Sheltie resembles a small Collie. The long-haired Collie type is required by the standard; short-haired dogs are not eligible for breeding. The Sheltie, like the Collie, is divided into groups according to the colour of the coat: sable (3), blue merle or tricoloured, black with tan and white markings (1). Black and tan (2) or black and white are also recognised. The nose must always be black, the eyes dark brown; only in the case of blue merles may the eyes be blue.

Bearded Collie (4)
Height: dog 53–56 cm, bitch 51–53 cm.
Weight: not prescribed. The colour may
be any shade of grey, black, blue
reddish-fawn, brown or sand, with or
without tan markings.

4

1

The Husky is a very old breed originating from Siberia. For the Chuckchi, a people who lived in the valley of the Kolyma River, these dogs were probably their most prized possessions. The Huskies guarded their property, pulled sleighs and accompanied hunters and children. Unlike other breeds of northern working dogs Siberian Huskies were often allowed inside their owners' dwellings. The breed became extremely popular in Europe in the mid-1920s. In the winter of 1925 Nome, Alaska, then a gold-miners' community, was struck by an epidemic of diphtheria and it was necessary to get serum there as quickly as possible. The Norwegian-born Leonhard Seppala and his team of Siberian Huskies covered 300 km in a blizzard and arrived with the medicine in the nick of time. Held every year in memory of this feat is the longest existing dog-sled race, called the Iditerod, covering a distance of 1,930 km from Anchorage to Nome. The Husky is a friendly dog, responsive to training and an excellent companion, whose popularity is continually on the increase, particularly in recent years.

Husky is also the name given to Eskimo dogs found in Greenland, Labrador, Alaska and northern Canada, but the correct name for this breed is Eskimo Dog. This breed originated and was recognised as a separate breed by the FCI only recently, with Canada as its place of origin. Unlike the Siberian Husky, the Eskimo Dog is distrustful and does not bark, but howls like a wolf. It is an excellent working dog, however, which not only pulls sleds but is also a good dog for hunting.

2

Siberian Husky (1)
Height: dog 53–60 cm, bitch 51–56 cm.
Weight: dog 20–27 kg, bitch 16–23 kg.
Colour: the colouring may be of any kind. Commonest are various shades of grey, tan, and black with white markings or patches. The dark crown and white 'spectacles' are typical. The eyes are brown or blue; eyes each of a different colour are allowed but are undesirable.

Eskimo Dog (2)
Height: dog 58–68 cm, bitch 51–61 cm.
Weight: dog 34–38 kg, bitch 27–31 kg.
Colour: unimportant; most frequent is white, black, black and white, wolf-colour, blue, tan, yellow-brown, or any combination of these colours. There are usually white or tan markings above the eyes.

1

3

Both breeds have thick pads on the feet which are further protected by long hair and thick skin between the toes (3).

Swiss Mountain Dogs

Swiss mountain dogs are descended from Roman dogs. In the remote valleys of the Swiss Alps where even the people remained relatively isolated, these dogs developed into separate breeds identical in their characteristic colouring but differing in size and coat, and sometimes also the shape of the tail. The largest is the Great Swiss Mountain Dog which was often used to haul light carts. Then the breed slowly but surely began to disappear and it was only at the beginning of the twentieth century that renewed interest on the part of dog breeders saved it from extinction.

The most popular of the Swiss mountain dogs is, without doubt, the Bernese Mountain Dog, differing from all the others in its soft, long coat. It is the most widely bred of the four breeds, not only in Switzerland but elsewhere as well. The Appenzell Mountain Dog is a medium-sized breed developed in the Toggenburg valley, round St Gall and in Appenzell Canton. At first glance it differs from the other Swiss mountain dogs in that its tail is carried curled above the back. The last of the four breeds is the Entlebuch Mountain Dog from the cantons of Lucerne and Berne. Its tail is congenitally short.

All Swiss mountain dogs are intelligent, faithful and good watchdogs. They are used as working dogs for guarding and herding flocks, as well as rescue dogs in the event of avalanche. They are readily trained. Because they are such handsome dogs they are also kept as housedogs, particularly the Bernese Mountain Dog. The Great Swiss Mountain Dog is expecially good with children. The very lively Entlebuch Mountain Dog requires plenty of exercise and is therefore less suitable for the household, the same being true of the naturally vigorous Appenzell Mountain Dog.

Great Swiss Mountain Dog (1)
Height: dog 66–71 cm, bitch 61–66 cm.
Weight: dog 52–58 kg, bitch 50–55 kg.

Bernese Mountain Dog (2)
Height: dog 64–70 cm (ideally 66–68 cm), bitch 58–66 cm (ideally 60–63 cm). **Weight:** not officially prescribed.

2 ♂

3 ♂

4 ♂

1 ♂

Entlebuch Mountain Dog (4)
Height: 40–50 cm – dog up to 56 cm, bitch up to 51 cm. **Weight:** not officially prescribed.

Colour the same for all four breeds: black with red markings on the cheeks, above the eyes and on all four legs, and with a white blaze, white feet, white tip of the tail, and white cross on the breast. The inner thighs, underside of the tail and inside of the ears should be red.

Appenzell Mountain Dog (3)
Height: dog up to 60 cm, bitch up to 55 cm. **Weight:** of no consequence.

Welsh Corgis and Swedish Vallhund

The Welsh Corgis are very old breeds of small, short-legged herding dogs from Wales, known there since the tenth century. In all probability they are descended from dogs brought to the British Isles in Viking ships. These small dogs were used to guard flocks of sheep, cattle and ponies. Since time immemorial there have been two types of these dogs in Wales. The first, slightly smaller type had a rudimentary tail or was tailless, the second was somewhat larger with a fox-like tail held straight out. It was not until 1925 that these dogs began to appear in shows, but the two types were not separated. In 1928 Welsh Corgis were registered as a breed by the English Kennel Club. Later the two types began to be bred separately.

As of 1934, each has its individual standard and crossing of the two is prohibited. The slighter, tailless type is called the Pembroke Welsh Corgi and the heavier type with the fox-like tail is called the Cardigan Welsh Corgi. The two also differ in other respects. The Pembroke Corgi has a more pronounced stop, more oval feet and, as a rule, a slightly longer coat.

Welsh Corgis are amiable, intelligent dogs and very good with children. The Cardigan Corgi is calmer than the extremely lively Pembroke Corgi. There has been a continued increase in the popularity of both breeds in recent years.

In Sweden there is an interesting breed of dog which exhibits a marked resemblance to the Welsh Corgi – the Swedish Vallhund or Västgötaspets, a favourite of farmers and shepherds. It is faithful and courageous and a very good watchdog. In all probability, its ancestry likewise goes back to the dogs of the Vikings.

Pembroke Welsh Corgi (1)
Height: 25—31 cm. **Weight:** 10—12 kg.
Colour: generally solid red, reddish-brown, sable, fawn, or black and tan; other colour mixtures with white prevailing are allowed, as are white markings on the legs, neck and chest.

Cardigan Welsh Corgi (2)
Height: dog 30 cm, bitch 27 cm. **Weight:** in proportion to size. **Colour:** all colours except pure white are allowed.

3

Swedish Vallhund (3)
Height: dog 33–35 cm, bitch 31–33 cm.
Weight: 9–14 kg. **Colour:** grey with
black-tipped hairs, reddish-yellow,
greyish-brown, brindle or irregularly
blotched blue and grey. A few white
markings are allowed.

Some breeds of short-legged dogs
have the forearm slightly curved inward.
The Pembroke Welsh Corgi, Cardigan
Welsh Corgi and Vallhund must have
straight legs with elbows lying close to
their sides.

UTILITY DOGS

Boston Terrier and Miniature Bull Terrier

The Boston Terrier is one of the few American breeds which has gained widespread popularity. It was developed in the second half of the nineteenth century in and around Boston, Massachusetts, by crossing the coloured Bull Terrier, the English Bulldog and the French Bulldog. By appearance one would definitely not think to class it among the terriers; most of its features seem to have come from its bulldog forebears. The first standard was set up in 1891, although at that time the dogs were still called by various names. Not until later did the present name of Boston Terrier become permanently established.

The Boston Terrier is often designated as one of the most pleasant of companions. It is very intelligent, amiable, a good dog for keeping in the house, playful and friendly and an extremely wary and courageous watchdog.

In early litters of Bull Terriers there often appeared pups which were small and light and thus unsuitable for the dog fights that were so popular at the time. In the late nineteenth century selective breeding of these small Bull Terriers produced a breed called the Miniature Bull Terrier, which was extremely popular as a companion dog at the beginning of the twentieth century. Later, however, its popularity waned until it was nearly on the verge of extinction and thus it is rarely encountered nowadays. The Miniature Bull Terrier is classified as a terrier by the British Kennel Club, not as a utility dog.

2 ♂

Boston Terrier
Height: 35–45 cm. **Weight:** should not exceed 11.4 kg. The Boston Terrier is divided into three categories according to weight: lightweight, under 6.8 kg; middleweight 6.8–9.1 kg; heavyweight 9.1–11.4 kg. **Colour:** in all weight categories brindle or black (1) with symmetrical white markings: a white nose, blaze, breast and throat, collar and legs. Boston Terriers are born with a short, rudimentary tail which should not be docked. They have prick ears.

74

Miniature Bull Terrier (2)
Height: not more than 35.5 cm. **Weight:**
no limit. **Colour:** as for the Bull Terrier
(p. 100) — white, black brindle, red, fawn
and tricolour.

1 ♀

The existence of this breed in China is recorded from more than 4,000 years ago. Statuettes of dogs dating from the Hau dynasty are unequivocally dogs of this breed. Their origin should probably be looked for in Manchuria where the Chow Chow was used for hunting. In northern China it was used for pulling loads and also raised for its fur. Besides this it was used as a watchdog throughout the whole of China.

The Chow Chow was first brought to Europe in 1887, when the Earl of Londsdale presented one as a gift to his bride. The dog's interesting appearance caught the fancy of all who saw it and the Chow Chow soon became the fashion of the day. Besides its pleasing looks, it also has a unique disposition. It is calm, non-aggressive and absolutely fearless. It is very independent and averse to training, although it instinctively understands its owner's wishes and fulfils these if it has absolute faith in him or her. It is not a dog to be played with and is definitely not suitable as a companion for children.

The Chow Chow belongs to the group of Asian spitzes which were used mostly for hunting. Several of these breeds are native to Japan and the forebears of some definitely include the Smooth-coated Chow Chow. The largest of these Japanese breeds is the Akita-Inu, whose pedigree may be traced as far back as the year 1500. This immensely strong dog was used as a watchdog, for pulling loads and also for hunting bear and deer. It requires a firm hand when being trained.

2

Chow Chow
Height: dog 48–56 cm, bitch 46–51 cm.
Weight: 18–25 kg. **Colour:** red, blue, fawn (1), black (2), cream, white. The last two are very rare. The coat is profuse, dense, straight and stands away from the body. The primary hairs are coarse to the touch, the undercoat is soft and woolly. Less common is the Short-haired Chow Chow with primary hairs less than 4 cm long and without a mane.

Akita-Inu (3)
Height: 51–68.5 cm. **Weight:** 54–60 kg.
Colour: deer-red, white, wheaten, black, grey-brown, ash-grey, silvery, steel-blue, black and tan, or brindle. The coat is hard, straight and stands away from the body; the undercoat is soft and woolly.

3

1

Although the FCI recognises the Dalmatian as a Yugoslavian breed, its origin is not quite clear. It is a known fact that these dogs were kept and bred in Dalmatia as early as the thirteenth century, but the Zadar town chronicle of 1822, for example, speaks of them as Danish dogs. Originally Dalmatians were hunting dogs, although they are no longer used for hunting.The English breeders who brought Dalmatians to England in 1862, spoke of them as dogs of the Dalmatian frontier guard. In the seventeenth century they were always part of the papal cortège; in the eighteenth they served primarily as impressive adjuncts accompanying horseback riders as well as carriages in France and England. Nowadays Dalmatians are used exclusively as companion dogs, although attempts were made in the United States to train them for police work. The Dalmatian is a calm dog, readily trained and suspicious of strangers. It acquired its present external appearance in England, where its development was influenced mainly by the Pointer.

In the eighteenth century the Dalmatian was often called the Bengali Bracke. Even though present-day authorities claim that the Dalmatian is not of Asian origin, there is no denying the fact that like-coloured hounds existed in Asia. Similarly coloured, for example, was the now extinct Russian Harlequin Hound, forebear of the Dunker, a Norwegian breed of hound developed at the beginning of the nineteenth century, mainly for hunting hares.

2 ♂

Dalmatian
Height: dog 58.4–61 cm, bitch 55.9–58.4 cm. **Weight:** 23–25 kg. **Colour:** white with sharply defined round black (1) or liver-brown spots, 20—30 mm in diameter. The spots on the head, ears, tail and legs should be smaller than those on the body. The nose of black-spotted dogs should always be black, in brown-spotted dogs it should always be brown. The eyes of black-spotted dogs should be black or brown, those of brown-spotted dogs should be amber or tinged with brown.

1 ♀

Dunker
Height: 47–57 cm. **Weight:** 18–20 kg.
The dogs are bred in three **colours:** blue
marbled or harlequin (2), black, and
chestnut-brown. White markings are
permissible in marbled dogs but they
must not predominate.

Since the thirteenth century fights between dogs and bulls (so-called bull-baiting) were frequently held in England. This sport reached the height of its popularity between the 1300s and the 1500s. The proclaimed victors were those dogs which succeeded in sinking their teeth into the bull's nose and hanging on until the bull stopped putting up a fight. From Mastiffs, small dogs were bred with broad faces, a marked undershot bite and greatly shortened muzzles which aided the dog in breathing while the teeth held fast in a tight grip. Descriptions of these dogs from as far back as 1631 correspond to the basic characteristics laid down by the present standard for the Bulldog. Today's Bulldog is only slightly lower and heavier than the dogs of that time.

In 1835 all animal fights were prohibited by law, violation of which was punishable by high fines. Fighting dogs of all kinds gradually disappeared from the scene. The English Bulldog only survived through the efforts of several people with a business-like turn of mind who hoped that the prohibition of fighting would be revoked after a time and so continued to breed these dogs. Systematic breeding of the Bulldog was not initiated until 1864, however, and was further developed after the founding of the Bulldog Club Incorporated, in 1875.

The previously required biting ability and pugnacious traits of the Bulldog were intentionally suppressed in later breeding and that is why today's Bulldog is good-natured, affectionate and loyal to all members of the family as well as amiable towards other domestic animals. Only rarely can the Bulldog be provoked to fight, but when it does it always comes away the victor. The Bulldog barks very little and does not need much exercise. This, too, makes it an ideal dog for the household.

2 ♂

Height: 40 cm. **Weight:** dog 25 kg, bitch 22.7 kg. **Colour:** any colour except black, black and tan, and black and white. Dogs of a solid colour have a dark mask. The eyes should be as dark as possible and should not show any white when the dog is looking straight ahead. The English Bulldog (1) has a broad body with a roach (slightly dipping) back (2), a muscular neck with a lobe of skin on each side, and slightly longer hind legs, so that the region of the loins is higher than the shoulders. The shape of the Bulldog's ear is also typical (3). It is a relatively small, thin, rose-shaped ear with inner folds directed backwards, thereby exposing the greater part of the inside of the lobe.

The Bulldog has an unusual, heavy and laborious gait because it takes short quick steps on the tips of its toes. The hind legs move just above the ground.

3

1 ♀

French Bulldog

The controversy over whether this breed is of French or English origin is one of long standing. The French claim that it is a breed developed from a small Mastiff by the breeding-in of small Griffons, Brabançons and Pugs; the English consider it to be descended from the Toy Bulldogs kept mainly by weavers around Nottingham. In 1850 some weavers and lacemakers emigrated from there to Normandy, purportedly taking Toy Bulldogs with them. Because further records state that these small bulldogs were crossed with indigenous bulldogs, the truth is probably somewhere in between. Be this as it may, the FCI recognised the French Bulldog or Bouledogue Français as a French breed.

The French Bulldog is an intelligent, lively dog which is fond of children. It barks very little and so is very suitable for town apartments. It does require quite a lot of exercise, however. Breeding and raising these dogs has its problems. The French Bulldog does not stand up well to hot weather; the shortened nose sometimes causes respiratory problems; the pups have a relatively large head and thus whelping is not always a simple matter, often requiring the administrations of a vet. Despite all this the French Bulldog has retained its popularity. It is a good companion and watchdog, and lots of fun – its happy nature and playfulness make it the darling of the family.

2 ♂

Height: 25–34 cm. **Weight:** dog 12–17 kg, bitch 10.9 kg. **Colouring** is of three kinds. Brindle (1) is a mixture of black and coloured hairs which are not too dark; a small amount of white is permissible on the head and breast. Pied (2) consists of brindle spots or patches on a white ground. Fawn may have brindle hairs. The eye rims and eyelashes of all types should be black; there must not be any unpigmented spots on the face. Very occasionally a dog may be pure white, but such dogs must have the black eye rims and eyelashes. At shows white dogs are judged in the pied group. The nose must always be black and broad with spreading nostrils. A nose with narrow nostrils is undesirable because then the dog snores loudly. The coat should be short, smooth, close-lying and fine. The tail is either vestigial or short and set low, thick at the root, knobbly or with a sideways kink and thin at the tip; it is always held below the level of the back.

1 ♀

When Marco Polo wrote in 1295 about his experiences in China he also mentioned the dogs he saw there. From his detailed descriptions we can recognise the Tibetan Mastiff and the Lhasa Apso. Perhaps their number also included other breeds, for even nowadays, for example, it is not easy to distinguish the Lhasa Apso from the Shih-Tzu. Some authorities are of the opinion that the Lhasa Apso originated through the crossing of the Tibetan Terrier and the Tibetan Spaniel, but according to others it is a native Chinese breed which made its way to Tibet at a later date. The fact remains, however, that scholars who came to Tibet in the twentieth century found these small dogs mainly in Tibetan monasteries, where they guarded the treasures of Buddha. The first standard for the Lhasa Apso was not set up until 1934; however the possibility that it may have been confused with other Tibetan dogs prior to that time cannot be ruled out.

While the Lhasa Apso fulfilled its duties in monasteries, a slightly larger, shaggy dog of somewhat similar appearance watched over herds of yaks in the Tibetan mountains. This typical herding dog, which many view as the forebear of the Puli, was named Tibetan Terrier by the British, although it has nothing to do with terriers. Even its character is quite different; it is not excitable like the terriers. Although its coat requires regular, thorough care, the Tibetan Terrier has become a popular companion dog wherever it has been introduced outside its native land.

2

Lhasa Apso
Height: 25.5 cm. **Weight:** 5–7 kg. **Colour:** any colour, but preference is given to golden, sandy, honey (1), dark grizzle, smoke, slate-grey, black, white, brown and part-coloured. An important ornamental feature of this breed is the long hair on the head which forms a cascade falling over the eyes, whiskers and beard. The hair on the ears is long and profuse, as is the hair on the tail, which should be carried high over the back. A low-set tail is a grave fault.

1

Tibetan Terrier
Height: dog 35–40.6 cm, bitch 32–35 cm.
Weight: up to 15 kg. **Colour:** white,
golden, cream, smoke-grey, black,
part-coloured or tricoloured (2).
Chocolate-brown or liver colouring
is not acceptable.

Poodles

This ancient breed, one of the oldest, is the subject of controversy as to its place of origin. The Germans claim the Poodle is a German breed; the French consider it to be a French breed. In the end the FCI recognised it as a French breed and the French were made responsible for setting the standard. Originally Poodles were hunting dogs used mainly for hunting water game, as borne out by both the German and French names. The old German 'Pfudel' means puddle, the French 'Caniche' is derived from *canard*, meaning duck. It is interesting to note that the coats of Poodles had apparently been trimmed since early times. Conrad Gesner, in his *Historia Animalium* of 1551, writes of water dogs trimmed in the manner of a lion.

The Poodle has a copious, fine, woolly, curly coat that is dense and of equal length all over. Trimming the coat is a very exacting task and begins as early as four months of age. Poodles have been bred in various sizes. Toy Poodles were already kept as pets at the court of Louis XVI.

Poodles are considered to be among the most intelligent of dogs. Nowadays they are no longer used for hunting but kept only as companion dogs.

3

Height: Standard Poodle (1) over 38 cm, Miniature Poodle (2) 28–38 cm, Toy Poodle under 28 cm. **Weight:** Standard Poodle 30 kg, Miniature Poodle 5–7 kg, Toy Poodle maximum 5 kg. **Colour:** in all Poodles black, warm dark brown, silver, blue, apricot (2), white (1). Pups of silver Poodles are born black and gradually become lighter up until the sixteenth week.

At the age of six months pups are generally given a 'lamb cut', i.e. the coat is clipped symmetrically over the whole body to a length of 1–2 cm. Sometimes pups are given a 'baby cut', which is a more or less modified version of the standard cuts. Adult poodles being trimmed for showing should have the classical trim or lion cut (1). Other styles are the modern trim (2) and the so-called Dutch trim (3).

1

2

The origin of the Standard Schnauzer is not quite clear but we do know that there were similar dogs in medieval days, mainly in Würtemberg. The present Standard Schnauzer-type dog was not developed until the beginning of the twentieth century when the Schnauzerklub was founded in 1907. Previously Schnauzers were used as trustworthy companions of waggoners and as watchdogs; nowadays they are popular for their lively but unexcitable disposition, fearlessness and tirelessness. Because the Schnauzer is not much given to barking unnecessarily, it is also a good dog for city dwellers. Care must be devoted to its coat, which is plucked on various parts of the body according to an established pattern.

In southern Bavaria, Salzburg and in the Tyrol at one time, large rough-haired dogs were kept to guard pigs and cattle and to defend farms against thieves. They were first exhibited in 1909 in Munich, and in 1923 they received their first official standard. This is a breed of large dog called the Giant Schnauzer, used nowadays practically only as service dogs. The Giant Schnauzer is self-confident, relatively fierce and wary of strangers, and is an excellent guard dog. Its vitality and need for plenty of exercise, however, make it a dog that is not suitable for everybody.

The late nineteenth century saw the development of the Miniature Schnauzer, bred by crossing smaller offspring of the Standard Schnauzer and the Affenpinscher. Although this is a miniature breed, these small dogs are endowed with the same abilities as their larger relatives and are classed as service dogs. Because of its happy disposition and simple requirements, the Miniature Schnauzer is becoming increasingly popular as a companion dog.

Standard Schnauzer (3)
Height: 45–50 cm. **Weight:** 15–18 kg.
Colour: black or pepper and salt (1). Permissible are shades ranging from steel-grey to silver-grey, always with a darker mask and grey undercoat.
Giant Schnauzer (2)
Height: dog 65–70 cm, bitch 60–65 cm. **Weight:** 35–50 kg. **Colour:** black or pepper and salt. Nowadays, however, pure black dogs are bred almost exclusively.

Miniature Schnauzer (4)
Height: 30–35 cm. **Weight:** not officially
prescribed but the dogs must look
proportional. **Colour:** black, pepper and
salt, or black-silver. Pepper and salt
colouring may be in shades ranging
from steel-grey to silver-grey with a grey
undercoat and darker mask; black-silver
colouring has a black outercoat as well
as undercoat and white markings above
the eyes, on the cheeks, chest, feet and
round the anus.

1 ♀

Dogue de Bordeaux, Shar-Pei and Portuguese Shepherd Dog

The Dogue de Bordeaux is a very old French breed related to the Mastiffs and descended from the Roman Molossus dogs. The Dogue de Bordeaux was bred and used in southern France as a courageous fighter of bears and wolves. From southern France it made its way to Spain and thence with the conquistadores to America, where it acquired a bad reputation as a vicious beast in battles against the Indians. As the result of selective breeding, however, the present-day Dogue de Bordeaux has many positive characteristics and its rapacity and aggressiveness have now been suppressed. It is an excellent watchdog and good with children, but often aggressive towards other dogs. It finds it difficult to adapt to a change of owner.

Descended from the ancient Mastiffs is the Shar-Pei breed, listed in the 1978 *Guiness Book of Records* as the rarest dog in the world, which has existed in China for more than 2,000 years. The Chinese used it to watch over herds of grazing cattle and to defend them against predators. The Shar-Pei has typical loose skin arranged in numerous folds and covered with one of two types of hairs. The first type is short and hard and is called 'horse' hair, the second type is about 2.5 cm long and stands away from the body at a 90-degree angle – this is called 'bristle' hair. Puppies are born with a short tail, as if it were docked, a medium-long tail or a long tail. The tail always curls up over the back.

Portugal, more precisely the Alentejo province, is the home of another dog related to the Mastiffs. It is called the Cao Rafeiro do Alentejo, or Portuguese Shepherd Dog, and is a self-confident, aggressive guard of herds.

3 ♂

Dogue de Bordeaux (1)
Height: 58–60 cm. **Weight:** dog at least 45 kg, bitch at least 40 kg. **Colour:** all shades of yellow-red, dogs with a dark mask are preferred.

Shar-Pei (2)
Height: 46–51 cm. **Weight:** 18–25 kg. **Colour:** red, fawn, cream or black. The typical skin with its numerous folds requires regular wiping with a damp sponge. Dogs from China have a narrower skull than dogs from Hong Kong.

Portuguese Shepherd Dog (3)
Height: dog 66–73.5 cm, bitch
63.5–69 cm. **Weight:** not officially
prescribed. **Colour:** black, wolf-grey,
fawn or yellow, with white markings on
the head, neck, legs and tail, or white
with markings in the aforesaid colours.

2

1

The Shih-Tzu is probably a Tibetan dog which originated from crossing the Lhasa Apso and the Pekingese; some authorities also believe the Tibetan Terrier may have figured in its origin. This vagueness is caused primarily by the fact that so-called 'lion dogs' were kept in both China and Tibet in ancient times, this name designating merely the external appearance, not a specific breed. The origin of this group of dogs is explained by a legend according to which Buddha was always accompanied by small lions which, when danger threatened, instantly grew larger and protected their master. 'Lion dogs' may thus have been Pekingese, just as well as Shih-Tzus or Lhasa Apsos.

Unlike other small breeds from this region, the Shih-Tzu arrived in Europe at a relatively late date. The first breeding pair was brought to England in 1930. In its native land the Shih-Tzu is kept as a watchdog, but in Europe as well as the USA, where it was not known until 1960, it is kept exclusively as a pet.

The Shih-Tzu is intelligent, lively and likeable. It is quite self-confident and in some ways slightly reminiscent of the Dachshund.

Height: maximum of 26.7 cm. **Weight:** 4.5–7.3 kg. **Colour:** all colours but a white-tipped tail and white blaze on the forehead (1) are highly prized in part-coloured dogs. Dogs should have a black nose but in dogs with a liver coat the nose may be coloured dark liver.

The coat is long and dense but not wavy and with a good undercoat. The hair on the head is long, falling over the eyes and forming whiskers on the cheeks and sides of the muzzle. On the top of the muzzle it grows straight upwards and should resemble a chrysanthemum blossom. In its native land the hair on the head of the Shih-Tzu is dishevelled, however in the West it has become the custom to comb the thick, long hair up onto the top of the head and tie it with a ribbon thus showing to advantage the short, square muzzle and wide-spaced, large, round, dark brown eyes, which must not be protuberant.

1

TERRIERS

Airedale Terrier and Black Terrier terriers

The Airedale, originally called the Broken-haired Terrier, was developed in the valley of the River Aire in Yorkshire by crossing the Old English Terrier with the Otterhound and Welsh Harrier. The original type was not uniform either in size or colouring. Not until 1884 was the first standard laid down, according to which the breed was made uniform. In the beginning the Airedale Terrier was used for hunting, mainly for otters. Soon, however, it was discovered to be endowed with a wide variety of working qualities and it was put to use in police, communication and health work. In Europe the Airedale was the most widely used dog for these services prior to the First World War, partly because of its successful participation in suppressing the Boxer Rebellion in China in 1900. Nowadays it is not used for hunting but its qualities and characteristics are continually put to good use as a service dog.

Dog breeders in the Soviet Union developed a special breed for military service, in which the Airedale Terrier played a prominent role. The Black or Russian Terrier, as the breed is called, was developed from two lines. The first is descended from the Airedale Terrier and Giant Schnauzer, the second by crossing the Giant Schnauzer and Rottweiler. From the first line the new breed inherited its fierceness, from the second its calm disposition. The outcome is a breed with a well-balanced disposition and very lively responses, aggressive towards strangers, hardy and resistant to all unfavourable conditions.

Airedale Terrier (1)
Height: dog 58–61 cm, bitch 56–59 cm.
Weight: should be commensurate with height and type and is usually around 20 kg. **Colour:** the head and ears, with the exception of the black marks on the sides of the head, should be tan, the ears darker. The legs should be tan as far as the thighs and elbows, the body black or dark grizzle. The coat should be stripped for shows. The back, nape, area between the ears, neck, shoulders and tail must be stripped down to the undercoat. The transition between the stripped and unstripped parts of the body must be uninterrupted and smooth.

2

1

Black (Russian) Terrier (2)
Height: dog 66–72 cm, bitch 64–70 cm.
Weight: about 40 kg. **Colour:** black
faintly tinged with grey. The hair on the
neck should form a collar.

The Bedlington Terrier was developed in northern England. Originally it was called the Rothbury Terrier and only later was it named after the old English town of Bedlington where the largest breeding centre was located. The standard, laid down in 1869, holds practically without change to this day. The Bedlington Terrier carries the blood of the Bull Terrier, Dandie Dinmont Terrier, Whippet and probably other breeds also. Anyone who sees the Bedlington Terrier at a show, with its coat trimmed in the usual way, would be hard put to believe that the breed was developed to hunt foxes, badgers and otters and that it is a keen dog with good hunting qualities. Nowadays, of course, the Bedlington Terrier is primarily a companion dog. Its coat is quite unusual. It is thick and linty and stands out from the skin, but is not harsh. On the head and cheeks it has a tendency to twist. It must be trimmed. In the early days of dog breeding it was forbidden to use knives or scissors for this purpose and the tips of the hairs were singed to the required length with a candle. Nowadays this rather odd and dangerous method is naturally no longer used and the coats of Bedlington Terriers are trimmed with clippers or scissor-trimmed through a comb.

Very typical is the manner in which the Bedlington Terrier moves, quite differently from the other breeds of terriers. At a slow pace its step is rather jerky, light and springy, but when running it does so like a Greyhound, using its whole body.

Height: about 41 cm; dogs may be slightly taller, bitches slightly smaller. **Weight:** 8–10.4 kg. **Colour:** blue (1), blue and tan, liver (2) or sandy. Dogs of different colours may be mated and are also judged together at shows. The colour of the eyes and nose depends on the colouring of the body. Blue Bedlington Terriers should have dark, almost black eyes, tan-coloured ones should have hazel-coloured eyes and nose.

Trimming the coat (3) is a relatively lengthy process; some parts of the body, e.g. the sides, should be trimmed with clippers about six weeks before a show. Three weeks before a show it is necessary to trim the feet and toes, and one week before a show the lower jaw, cheeks and throat, as well as the ears except for the tip; immediately prior to a show it is necessary to smooth away all sharp transitions and to model the whole body into the desired shape. Special care should be devoted to the head with its typical crest so that, seen from the front, it forms a long, narrow, blunt wedge.

2 ♂

1

3

This breed originated in the border country between England and Scotland and is apparently very old. Nothing more precise, however, is known about its ancestry. The Border Terrier has always been and still is a typical working dog used mainly to hunt foxes in difficult terrain. The thick skin, dense, wiry outercoat and close undercoat provide excellent protection against wounds. It must, furthermore, be a tireless dog and fast enough on its feet to keep up with a horse. It often ran with Foxhounds and drove foxes out of their lairs. The breed did not receive official recognition until 1920, but it never became widespread and is only rarely seen at shows in Europe.

The Glen of Imaal Terrier originated in the valley or glen of the same name in the County of Wicklow, Ireland. It is a breed of true working dogs, developed for the rough conditions of hunting fox and badger. It is not seen at shows. Some authorities consider it to be the same breed as the Soft-coated Wheaten Terrier, but the Glen of Imaal Terrier is smaller and its coat is less dense and slightly harder.

Both breeds are very attached to their owners, and are brave and fierce. The Border Terrier is more adaptable and is good with children. However, neither is really suitable as a housedog.

Border Terrier
Height: 25–30 cm. **Weight:** dog 5.9–7.1 kg, bitch 5.1–6.4 kg. **Colour:** red (1), wheaten, grizzle and tan or blue and tan. The coat is dense, wiry and has a close undercoat. The head of the Border Terrier is different from that of other terriers – it should look like that of an otter. The tail is not docked.

Glen of Imaal Terrier
Height: should not exceed 36 cm. **Weight:** about 8 kg. **Colour:** wheaten (2), blue or brindle. The coat is abundant and soft, generally wavy to curly. The puppies are born either wheaten or more often rusty or grey. They have a dark, usually black, mask and some have a black stripe on their backs. These markings gradually disappear as the puppies get older. The relatively highly set tail may be docked to one third of its length if wished.

1 ♂

This breed originated by crossing the English Bulldog with various breeds of terriers. Later other breeds were bred in as well. It is a breed developed for fighting. The characteristics required of it are calmness, courage, independence, a strong bite, a swift attack and the ability to tolerate pain. The Bull Terrier is a strong, self-confident dog whose training requires a firm hand and plenty of time. Afterwards, however, it is an excellent companion, faithful and affectionate to all members of the family and good with children. It does not seek out fights with other dogs but if provoked is a ruthless adversary. From its terrier forebears it inherited hunting abilities that were once used both for tracking as well as for hunting wild boar.

Besides the Bull Terrier, also developed for fighting was the similar but larger Staffordshire Bull Terrier, which was more like the original type. When dog fights were prohibited in England in 1835, its popularity declined and the Staffordshire Bull Terrier was threatened with extinction. Not until 1935 were efforts begun to save the breed. The Staffordshire Bull Terrier is said to be more tenacious, more courageous and more skilful than the Bull Terrier. It is gaining in popularity in Britain and is also appearing with increasing frequency in Europe. It is easier to train than the Bull Terrier, but needs more exercise.

2 ♂

Bull Terrier
There are no height or weight limits but average figures would be as follows. **Height:** 40–55 cm. **Weight:** 20–30 kg. **Colouring** is divided into two groups. White dogs must be pure white with markings permissible only on the head from the ears forward. In coloured dogs the colour must predominate over the white (1); brindle is preferred. The coat is short and flat on the taut skin throughout. The eyes are narow, slanting, triangular and black or the darkest possible brown. Typical is the head which, viewed in profile, should almost form an arc from the crest of the occiput to the nose. The more convex it is, the better.

Staffordshire Bull Terrier (2)
Height: 35.5–40.6 cm. **Weight:** dog
12.7–17 kg, bitch 10.9–15.4 kg. **Colour:**
all colours are permitted (e.g. red, fawn,
white, black, blue-grey), either solid
colours, brindle, or any combination of
these colours with white.

1

Dandie Dinmont Terrier

The Dandie Dinmont Terrier is a relatively old breed from the border country between England and Scotland. Its origin is not absolutely clear, although it is presumed to carry the blood of the Otterhound, Beagle and some rough-haired terriers. The breed already existed round 1700. Generally breeds are named after their place of origin or after the breeder who contributed most to their development but the name of this breed is taken from literature. In 1814 a novel by Sir Walter Scott was published, entitled *Guy Mannering*, which tells the story of a farmer and huntsman by the name of Dandie Dinmont, who kept a pack of these dogs, noted in particular for their excellent work in hunting vermin.

The Dandie Dinmont is skilful and brave and furnished with a strong set of teeth and a loud voice, making it possible to locate its whereabouts when it is digging undergroud. A typical characteristic of its build is that the hindlegs are a little longer than the forelegs, making the back low at the shoulders with a pronounced arch over the loins.

The Dandie Dinmont Terrier is an affectionate, playful dog with a happy expression. It is an excellent companion and at the same time a good working dog endowed with many instinctive talents so that it needs practically no special training. Its coat needs daily combing and regular brushing and regular, gradual, inconspicuous stripping.

Height: 20–28 cm. **Weight:** 8–11 kg.
Colour: either pepper and salt (1) or mustard. The pepper may range from a dark bluish-grey to a light silvery-grey. The head (crest) should be creamy white (the lighter the better), and the legs and feet slightly darker than the head but lighter than the body. Intermediate hues are preferred. The hair on the upper side of the tail is wiry and should be darker than that of the body, and also darker than that of the underside of the tail, which is softer. The hair gradually gets shorter towards the tip of the tail.

3

2

According to the standard the tail
should be carried curved like a Turkish
sabre.
   The coat is about 5 cm long, a
mixture of hard and soft hairs. The ears
have a tuft of long, light-coloured, silky
hairs at the tips up to 10 cm long. These
usually grow in between the first and
second years (2); they are absent in
puppies (3).

Fox Terriers were used as far back as the fourteenth century to accompany all packs of hounds in fox-hunting and also to work independently underground. The older type is the Smooth-haired Fox Terrier. Wire-haired Fox Terriers were developed much later (not until 1814) by Jack Rusell, a British breeder who devoted his efforts to breeding various wire-haired terriers. The Fox Terrier Club, founded in England in 1875, did not recognise these wire-haired terriers and so they did not begin to gain wider popularity until the year 1913, when the Wire Fox Terrier Association was founded and when stripping was legalised. Soon, however, the Wire-haired Fox Terrier ousted the Smooth-haired Fox Terrier from its top-ranking position because the stripping of the coat gave a smarter, more attractive appearance and the wiry coat provided better protection against the weather as well as against the teeth of vermin.

The Fox Terrier is a dog of outstanding hunting qualities, suitable not only for work underground but also above ground in tracing as well as pursuing quarry; it also likes to work in water. Whereas dogs which choke vermin are preferred in Europe, in England the dog must drive the game out of its hole so that the chase may continue.

When properly trained the Fox Terrier is obedient and readily controlled. It is a very lively, temperamental dog which is not particularly suitable as a house pet.

2 ♂

Height: dog a maximum of 39.5 cm, bitch proportionately smaller. **Weight:** dog in show condition 8.25 kg, bitch 7.25 kg. **Colour:** white must be predominant (1) otherwise the colour is unimportant. However, brindle, red, liver or slate markings are inadmissible.

The Smooth-haired Fox Terrier (2) has a straight, smooth coat that lies close to the body. The coat of the Wire-haired Fox Terrier is wiry with a tendency to twist. It should be so dense and firm that if it is spread apart with the fingers one cannot see the skin. The undercoat is shorter, softer and finer than the outercoat.

The coat of the Wire-haired Fox Terrier should be stripped (3). The hair on the legs and beard is not stripped as a rule, otherwise the hair should be 3–3.5 cm long on the back, 1–1.5 cm long on the sides of the body and sides of the neck, and only a few millimetres long on the head and ears. The

transition from one part of the body to
another should be inconspicuous and
because the hairs on the various parts of
the body grow at a different rate the
various sections should be stripped
gradually step by step.

3

1 ♀

This breed was developed in Bavaria around 1920 by crossing Smooth-haired and Wire-haired Fox Terriers, Welsh Terries, and Lakeland Terriers whose female offspring were then mated with a single sire of the Old English Broken-haired Terrier breed, thereby obtaining dogs with multi-purpose hunting qualities. They were enthusiastic and keen underground workers, noisy when following a scent, and very good at following blood tracks. They were used primarily in West Germany and Austria, later spreading also to other European countries. Their increasing popularity was also due in great measure to the great success of this breed at international underground work field trials where the performance of the German Hunting Terriers was much steadier than that of other breeds.

Working qualities have always been given priority for this breed and that is why quite a bit of leeway is permitted by the standard for the external appearance. Compared to the British breeds of terriers the German Hunting Terriers looks slightly out of balance. It body is more rectangular, the ears larger and set high on the head and the feet longer than in most British terriers.

The German Hunting Terrier is a lively, intelligent, fierce dog that is distrustful of strangers. It is playful and needs plenty of exercise. This is definitely a dog for huntsmen and is not suitable as a housedog.

2 ♂

Height: 30–40 cm. **Weight:** dog 9–10 kg, bitch 7.5–8.5 kg. **Colour:** black, dark brown, black-grey grizzle, with brown-red or yellow markings above the eyes, on the muzzle, chest, legs and feet. Some white on the breast and toes is permitted.

The coat of the German Hunting Terrier may be of two types. Rough-haired dogs (1) have a straight, dense, hard and harsh coat, smooth-haired dogs (2) have a smooth, coarse, dense but not short coat. It does not require extensive grooming as do the coats of British breeds of terriers.

1 ♀

Irish Terrier
and Soft-coated Wheaten Terrier

The Irish Terrier is a descendant of an old Irish breed of terrier which was crossed with the Black and Tan Terrier. Rigid selective breeding to obtain the desired type was begun in 1870 and three years later the breed was shown in Dublin. The Irish Terrier is a typical hunting dog, daredevil and excellent tracker, capable of following a scent for many kilometres. The courage with which it flings itself at an adversary on command is in surprising contrast to its affection for and loyalty to its owner and its friendly attitude towards children. Nowadays the Irish Terrier is generally kept as a companion dog and even so is not very common.

The Soft-coated Wheaten Terrier slightly resembles the Irish Terrier at first glance. This breed likewise has a very old ancestry and originated in Ireland, in Munster. According to some legends the forebears of this breed came there from wrecked Spanish ships of the Armada. However, the breed did not receive official recognition until 1943. The Soft-coated Wheaten Terrier is a friendly, lively dog, distrustful of strangers. Because of its lively temperament it is not particularly suitable as a housedog. It is, however, a working dog of multi-purpose qualities, suitable for hunting as well as guarding and defending property and cattle.

Irish Terrier
Height: dog 48 cm, bitch 46 cm. **Weight:** dog 12.2 kg, bitch 11.3 kg. **Colour:** solid red, deep wheaten (1) or red-wheaten. The coat is hard and wiry with a soft undercoat. This dog is groomed by stripping in the same manner as the Airedale Terrier.

Soft-coated Wheaten Terrier (2)
Height: 46–49.5 cm. **Weight:** 16–20.4 kg. **Colour:** solid wheaten. Puppies are born coloured wheaten, red or grey. They have a dark mask and often a dark stripe on the back; these markings, however, disappear with age. The coat is abundant and soft, wavy or curly. It does not require any special grooming, merely regular brushing and combing to remove grime. In Ireland the coat is sometimes trimmed as for the Kerry Blue Terrier. In England there is a type of this breed with a somewhat more abundant coat, which was also taken to Europe.

2 ♂

1

The origin of this breed must be looked for amongst the offspring of the red Irish Terrier which occasionally included a dark grey-blue pup. Such pups were selected for further breeding, with the breeding-in of Bedlington Terrier, Dandy Dinmont Terrier and possibly also Bull Terrier blood to obtain a stabilised type. The present blue type was first shown in 1922 in London at Crufts Dog Show. The original purpose of the Kerry Blue Terrier, also called the Irish Blue Terrier, was to guard estates and hunt foxes and badgers and possibly also otters and rabbits. Later the Kerry Blue Terrier tended to become more of a companion dog, especially in Europe, whereas in its native land emphasis is still laid on good working qualities.

The Kerry Blue Terrier is an affectionate, alert and easily controlled dog, although usually intolerant of other dogs. Because of its temperamental disposition, it requires a firm hand in training. The coat needs regular care. It should not be stripped but trimmed with clippers and scissors. Work on the soft, silky, profuse and wavy coat should begin two to six weeks before a show. Even if the dog is not being prepared for a show, the coat should not be allowed to grow too long, because then the dog loses the characteristic appearance prescribed by the standard.

Height: 46–48 cm. **Weight:** 15–17 kg.
Colour: blue-grey (1) with or without black-tipped hairs. The head, ears, tail and feet may be darker. Puppies are born black (2) or tinged with brown. At the age of eighteen months they should acquire the adult colouring. After eighteen months no colour other than blue is allowed, although a small white patch on the breast should not be penalised at shows. The eyes should be as dark a brown as possible and small. The nails must be black.

When grooming the coat it is important to emphasise the long, slender neck. The hair on the throat should be trimmed close with clippers and the hair on the nape left longer to underscore the line of the neck. The chest is made to look deeper by leaving the hair on the lower chest untrimmed. The hair on the forelegs should be combed to make the legs look as powerful as possible.

1

Lakeland Terrier

The Lakeland Terrier may be readily confused with the Welsh Terrier. The two breeds differ, however, in the shape of the head and in their colouring. The Lakeland Terrier has a shorter head and the tan colour has a golden tone. The breed originated in England's Lake District and is derived from the Black and Tan Terrier, which used to be called the Patterdale Terrier in these parts, and the Bedlington Terrier. Rigid selective breeding gave the breed its noble cast and fixed it to such a degree that it was recognised as a separate breed in 1928.

The Lakeland Terrier was originally bred for hunting, mainly for going underground to flush out foxes. It was often used with Foxhound packs in the chase. However, it can also work as a beater to chase game out of thickets and is also very good for work in water because the structure of its coat makes it waterproof. It is also becoming increasingly popular as a companion dog. Despite its innate sharpness, it is a friendly, affectionate and undemanding companion in the house. Like most terriers, however, it needs plenty of exercise. The dense, harsh coat needs to be groomed by stripping.

2 ♂

Height: 36.8 cm. **Weight:** 6.8–7.7 kg.
Colour: black and tan, blue with tan markings (1), red, wheaten (2), red and black grizzle, liver, blue or black. Small white patches on the chest and on the feet are permissible. The tan markings must have a golden tinge, red or dark tan markings are considered a flaw.

The coat is stripped approximately twice a year, in spring and autumn as a rule. The stripping is the same as for most rough-haired terriers, except that on the bridge of the muzzle the hair is left longer to emphasise the shape of the head (3). When working on the dog it is best to stand it on a table and comb it thoroughly. Then, holding the skin with the fingers of the left hand, slowly strip the loose coat with the thumb and forefinger of the right hand, pulling out the hair in small clumps in the direction in which it grows. Begin at the shoulders

and continue systematically in this time-consuming process across the back to the sides and on to the tail. Strip the throat carefully so that the neck has a graceful line. Groom the hair on the legs to give them the appearance of powerful pillars.

3

1 ♀

Manchester Terrier
and English Toy Terrier

This breed is descended from the old English black and tan Broken-haired Terrier and the English White Terrier and is probably the oldest purposely bred terrier. It was already known in the sixteenth century, but attained its greatest popularity in the nineteenth century when it was used to kill rats on a large scale in shops, warehouses and docks. In those days they even held rat-catching contests in which the winner was the dog that could kill the greatest number of rats in an arena in a given time. The breeder John Hulme, who added Whippet blood to the Manchester Terrier, deserves credit for endowing the breed with speed and dexterity.

Later its popularity in England waned and during the Second World War the Manchester Terrier was threatened with extinction – only eleven dogs which could be considered pure-blooded remained. However, some dog breeders saw to it that this characteristic breed, whose blood probably runs in the veins of all other terrier breeds, was saved and, as of 1952, the breeding base is once again assured. The Manchester Terrier is an excellent companion and watchdog. Its short, dense, glossy coat does not require any special care.

The year 1850 or thereabouts marked the appearance of the English Toy Terrier, a miniature breed derived from the Manchester Terrier and the smallest specimens of the Piccolo Levriero Italiano. It differs from the Manchester Terrier not only in size but also primarily in its V-shaped prick ears. It is a one-person dog and a good watchdog. This breed is classified as a toy dog, not a terrier, by the British Kennel Club.

3 ♂

Manchester Terrier (1)
Height: dog 40–41 cm, bitch 38 cm.
Weight: 4–8 kg. **Colour:** black with mahogany markings on the inside of the legs, breast and head. There must be pencilling on the toes, i.e. a black line on each toe, and a black mark above the toes.

The Manchester Terrier originally had its ears cropped (2). Dogs bred after the English Kennel Club prohibited cropping in the late nineteenth century had high-set ears with drooping tips. The ears continue to be cropped in some countries.

English Toy Terrier (3)
Height: 25–30 cm (preferably as close as possible to the bottom limit). **Weight:** 2.7–3.6 kg. **Colour:** as for the Manchester Terrier.

Miniature Bull Terrier: see p. 74.

2

1 ♀

115

These small, lively, friendly dogs were raised round Norfolk and Cambridge as far back as the year 1880. The breed was markedly affected following the year 1901 when the breeder Frank Jones brought small rat-catchers to Norfolk from Ireland. He had decided to develop a breed of small terriers, not much larger than the Yorkshire Terrier, but so fierce and brave that they would engage in a fight with a fox and so tireless as to keep up with a rider on horseback the whole day long – furthermore they were to be terriers with no white whatsover. For a long time the results were not uniform so that the breed did not receive official recognition until 1932. Originally two types were recognised, one with prick ears and one with drop ears, which were judged separately at shows. As of 1965 the English Kennel Club decided to consider the two types as two separate breeds and the one with drop ears was named the Norfolk Terrier. Some countries, e.g. the USA, did not accept this division and dogs of both types continue to be judged there under the name Norwich Terrier.

The coat of both breeds needs minimum trimming, done only to underscore the dog's typical characteristics. The quality of the coat may also be gradually improved by stripping.

Despite their fierceness both the Norfolk and Norwich Terriers are happy, playful and very companionable dogs.

2

Both breeds
Height: 25 cm. **Weight:** 5 kg. **Colour:** red, wheaten, black and tan or grizzle. The coat is wiry, straight and lies close to the body; on the head and ears it is shorter but forms prominent whiskers and eyebrows. The hair on the neck and shoulders is longer and in winter forms a sort of mane.

1

The head is reminiscent of a small
fox. The muzzle and forehead comprise
about one-third of the entire length of
the head, the skull is slightly rounded,
broad between the eyes and with a good
stop. Typical are the relatively large,
strong teeth which are an indication that
these small dogs can be powerful
adversaries. The two breeds differ only
in the shape of the ears. The Norwich
Terrier (1) has small prick ears; the
Norfolk Terrier (2) has drop ears.

This old breed of terrier originated in northern Scotland or in the Orkney Islands. According to some authorities similar dogs already existed here at the time of the Roman invasion of Britain, but these were larger and had shorter jaws. Similar dogs are also found in sixteenth-century paintings. The Scottish Terrier acquired its present appearance some 300 years later. Dogs of the present type appeared at the 1879 Crufts Dog Show but they had weaker jaws, a weaker skeleton, and their forelegs were not very straight. These drawbacks were soon righted, so that the first standard could be laid down in 1883, which also marked the founding of the Scottish Terrier Club.

The breed's popularity waxed and waned according to the fashion of the day; the last high was between the two world wars. Nowadays the Scottish Terrier is kept mainly as a pet, to the detriment of its hunting features; the broad, deep chest prescribed by the present standard is not particularly suited for a dog working in the close quarters of fox holes. The Scottish Terrier has a happy disposition, is a wary watchdog, somewhat hard-headed, but good with children. Despite its short legs it is a very active dog and its movements are light and smooth.

Height: 25.4 cm. **Weight:** 8.6–10.4 kg. **Colour:** deep black (1), wheaten or brindle (2), but without markings.

The coat is dense, hard to wiry, with a dense and soft undercoat. Grooming is quite demanding; some parts of the body should be clipped, others stripped, and all at various different times to emphasise the typical characteristics required by the standard (3), for instance, the depth of the chest, well-angled legs, etc. The neck, back, forelegs and tail are stripped in the same way as in most other terriers, while the hair on the upper thighs should be left fairly long. Abundant hair on the belly emphasises the compactness of the body. In black and dark brindle Scottish Terriers the throat, forehead, cheeks and area under the tail should be trimmed,

2

in light brindle and wheaten dogs the forehead should be stripped and the cheeks should be trimmed only if this will not affect the intensity of the colouring (the undercoat is not light-coloured). The transition from the smooth forehead to the thicker hair between the ears and on the upperside of the neck should be gradual.

3

1

The origin of the Sealyham Terrier can be clearly traced because the man who developed it, Captain John Edwards of Sealyham House in Pembrokeshire, kept very precise records. His aim was to obtain a small white hunting dog of a lively disposition which was brave, intelligent and readily controlled. To this end he crossed the Cheshire Terrier, which resembled the Bull Terrier, the Pembroke Welsh Corgi, the Dandie Dinmont Terrier and the Wire-haired Fox Terrier, and then, to fix the white colour, he bred in the West Highland White Terrier. The offspring were subjected to a strict selective process which focused primarily on hunting qualities. Dogs that would not enter a fox or badger hole at the age of seven months were killed. The breed received official recognition in 1911. Since that time the Sealyham Terrier has lost much of its fierce enthusiasm because it has been used mostly as a companion dog in which a calm disposition is given preference. Even though the standard nowadays requires hunting qualities and a sharp reaction to vermin, it likewise stresses an affectionate nature and the qualities of a good companion.

The youngest breed of terriers is the Bohemian Terrier, officially recognised by the FCI in 1963. This breed was developed by crossing the Sealyham Terrier and the Scottish Terrier, with the aim of obtaining a good dog for work underground with a coat that does not need complex care. The Bohemian Terrier also has excellent qualities as a companion, has a calm nature and is good with children.

Sealyham Terrier
Height: 27–31 cm. **Weight:** 8–9 kg.
Colour: white (1), either all white or with yellow, yellow-brown, or badger-pied markings on the head and ears. The feet should have black pads. The coat is hard and wiry with a dense, soft undercoat. It should be groomed by stripping.

Bohemian Terrier
Height: 27–35 cm. **Weight:** about 8 kg.
Colour: either grey-blue (2) or light coffee-brown. Grey-blue dogs are born black, light coffee-brown dogs are born chocolate-brown. In both instances yellow, grey or white markings are allowed on the head, neck, breast and belly, also on the lower parts of the legs and round the anus. However, the coloured markings must not exceed 20 per cent of the body area. The coat is thick, soft, silky and wavy. It is groomed by clipping (3). The hair on the front

2

part of the head is not clipped, leaving
a beard and moustache and long
eyebrows. The hair on the legs, breast
and belly is likewise not clipped. The
transition between the clipped and
unclipped areas must be smooth and
inconspicuous.

3

1

The Skye Terrier comes from the Isle of Skye, one of the islands of the Inner Hebrides off the north-west coast of Scotland. Its forebears were short, long-haired dogs which have lived on the island since time immemorial. It is said that these dogs also carry the blood of spaniels which arrived there from off wrecked ships of the Spanish Armada. The Skye Terrier was used primarily to hunt foxes, badgers and otters but also as a watchdog. Nowadays, mainly because of the long silky coat prescribed by the standard, it is only rarely used for hunting. Skye Terriers may be of two types: with prick ears or with drop ears. Some countries allow mutual mating of the two types, others keep their pedigrees separate.

In Edinburgh there stands a stone fountain with a statue of the Skye Terrier, commissioned in 1872 in memory of the most faithful dog in the world, Greyfriar's Bobby, who kept a vigil for fourteen years at his master's grave until he himself died there. The Skye Terrier is truly undemanding, faithful and a good watchdog but definitely a one-person dog. It is often aggressive towards strangers.

Height: 25–26 cm. **Weight:** 11.3 kg. The Skye Terrier is a long-bodied dog – the body of the adult dog should be no less than 105 cm. **Colour:** generally black, dark blue-grey, light or dark silvery-grey, light grey (1) or fawn (2) with black-tipped hairs. The colour must be uniformly intense, but the fringe on the ears and muzzle must be nearly as dark as black. The extremely long (15 cm on average), hard outer coat must be straight; the undercoat is dense, soft, woolly and short. The hair on the head is softer than on the other parts of the body and covers the front of the head and eyes. Typical are the long, pendant hairs on the inner sides of the ears and the feathering on the tail. The Skye Terrier's coat is neither clipped nor stripped, however it must be brushed thoroughly every day, taking care not to tear out the hair unnecessarily.

Prior to a show or other event where the dog must be in perfect condition, bathe the dog the day before the event and, while it is still slightly damp, part the hair in a straight line along the back and comb it to each side (3). Then blow the hair dry with a hair drier, smoothing it down with a brush as you do so.

3

1

Welsh Terrier and Otterhound

The Welsh Terrier is one of the oldest breeds in the British Isles. It has been known and prized in Wales for centuries, mainly as a watchdog but also frequently used in hunting. Around the mountains and rivers of that region there was always plenty of game. The most popular forms of hunting were fox and otter hunts and so the small Welsh Terrier was teamed with the large Otterhound to run in the dog pack. The first such dog pack probably belonged to King John in 1212. Pedigree breeding of the Welsh Terrier did not begin, however, until the mid-nineteenth century. For a long time the breed was confined to the British Isles and it was only after 1920 that it found its way to Europe where it soon became a popular companion dog. However, its outstanding inherent hunting qualities, and above all its calm disposition, whereby it differed from the hitherto used Fox Terrier, soon made it highly prized by huntsmen.

The Welsh Terrier is temperamental but obedient and readily controlled and is good with children. Its small size, along with its dark colouring, make it an ideal dog for the city, where light-coloured dogs require frequent bathing. The profuse, hard, wiry, close-lying coat needs to be groomed by stripping.

Unlike the Welsh Terrier its hunting companion, the Otterhound, did not become a companion dog. It is a friendly and good-natured dog, which has a dense but rather greasy coat. The Otterhound is classified as a hound by the British Kennel Club.

Welsh Terrier (1)
Height: should be no more than 39 cm.
Weight: about 9–9.5 kg. **Colour:** black and tan or black-grizzle and tan (1); black below the hocks and on the toes is considered to be a fault.

Otterhound (2)
Height: dog approximately 67 cm, bitch 60 cm. **Weight:** 30–32 kg. **Colour:** various shades of blue and white, black and tan or brownish. The skin between the toes is webbed, enabling the dog to be a good swimmer.

2

1

West Highland White Terrier and Cairn Terrier

The West Highland White Terrier comes from the north-west Highlands of Scotland. At some time in the seventeenth century this breed was developed from white puppies which appeared in the litters of the small dogs raised in that region. These were useful hunting dogs in that they differed in colour from the quarry pursued by the huntsmen. In 1890 these attractive small dogs made their way from Scotland to England where they became very popular, particularly as pets. Breeding focused more on the aesthetic qualities of the dog's external appearance than on its hunting qualities and so nowadays the West Highland White Terrier is rarely encountered amongst huntsmen. It is a very good-natured companion however, brave, self-confident and a good watchdog which barks at any sign of danger.

The Cairn Terrier is probably a breed which figured in the ancestry of the West Highland White Terrier and that of the Scottish Terrier as well. This fierce pursuer of all vermin was previously considered to be merely a short-haired form of the Skye Terrier, until 1910, when the two were recognised as separate breeds. The Cairn Terrier takes its name from the cairns or heaps of boulders on Scotland's coast, dating perhaps from the days of the Celts, which often served as hiding places for foxes, otters and other predators. Cairn Terriers were the dogs best suited for work in this difficult terrain. Although they are now mainly popular as companion dogs, they continue to retain their excellent hunting qualities. In the house they are excellent watchdogs which do not bar unnecessarily.

2

West Highland White Terrier (1)
Height: about 28 cm. **Weight:** 7.5–8.5 kg.
Colour: pure white. The coat should be stripped. Before stripping the head, comb all the hair back to smooth it down; then, when it is combed forward, it will stand up straight and the longest hairs to be plucked out can be more readily grasped. The hair on the cheeks should first be combed downward and then upward. The hair on the head must be short enough to emphasise the shortness and breadth of the head. The front part of the whiskers and the hair on the muzzle should be stripped so that when the hair is combed back the dog looks as if it is running against the wind (2).

126

3

Cairn Terrier (3)
Height: 28–31 cm. **Weight:** 6–7.5 kg.
Colour: red (3), cream, grey, brindle or
almost black. Darker ears and a darker
nose are typical.

1

HOUNDS

Afghan Hound hounds

The native land of this magnificent hound is Afghanistan and the frontier regions of southern China and Kashmir. It is a very ancient breed which already existed in 2000 BC and remained purebred. Emphasis was naturally placed more on its working qualities than on its appearance. The Afghan Hound was used not only for hunting but also for herding and as a watchdog. In Afghanistan there are two types: a smaller, more temperamental mountain type sometimes called Ghazni, and a larger, heavier plainland type sometimes called Bell Murrey after the Englishman who first brought it to Europe in 1888. The standard for the breed was set up according to the mountain type. Imports in ensuing years, mainly in 1920–24, included both types, which also differ slightly in the structure of the coat, and this gave rise to disputes. The new standard of 1925, however, was again based on the Ghazni type and so the Bell Murrey type gradually vanished from the scene.

The Afghan Hound is self-confident, distrustful of strangers, seemingly peaceful, but showing the full force of its temperament when in action. It is a dog which requires plenty of exercise. Quite a lot of attention must be devoted to its long, silky coat, which must be combed and brushed daily.

2

Height: dog 68–74 cm, bitch 63–69 cm. **Weight:** 25–30 kg. **Colour:** all colours are acceptable. Most common are yellow-brown (1) with a dark mask, greyish-red, and black and tan (2). The coat is long, silky and fine on the flanks, breast and hind-quarters; on the back from the shoulders to the root of the tail it is short and very dense. On the head from the forehead backwards it forms a long silky topknot; on the face it is short and thick. The ears and legs are covered with long, profuse hair. For practical reasons the feathering on the feet is trimmed.

The Afghan Hound has a typical stance and gait. The head is carried high and proudly, the dog's movements are springy and supple, underscored further by the movement of the coat. The dog should give the impression of strength and dignity combined with speed and power.

1

This breed is descended from a group of primitive dogs living semi-wild in Africa and Asia. As a rule no one pays any attention to such dogs, nor even feeds them, and that is why the name pariah dog used to be applied to them all collectively. More recently canine authorities have classed them in the Schensi-Hunde group. Several of these dog groups formed stable types currently recognised as separate breeds, and one of the most typical is the Basenji, which originated in central Africa, northern Zaire and southern Sudan.

In their countries of origin these dogs are used to help in hunting game, as rodent killers, and to flush smaller species of antelope, e.g. duikers. There are two types of Basenji: a smaller, darker type found in virgin forests and a larger, lighter-coloured type found in more open country where savanna is interspersed with bush. There are, naturally, transitional types between the two, e.g. dogs found in the region of the upper Uellé River.

Basenjis were occasionally brought to Europe and America as curiosities. They did not acclimatise well, however, and attempts to breed them failed. Not until the late 1930s did breeders succeed in raising several litters and since then the Basenji has occasionally been seen at shows.

2 ♂

Height: of the forest type about 40 cm, of the savanna type about 43 cm.
Weight: 9–11 kg. **Colour:** chestnut, black, black and tan (1); dogs from the Sudan savannas are usually flaxen. Typical features are the large white patch on the breast extending in the form of a broad collar round the neck, the white feet and the white tip of the tail. A white blaze on the forehead is allowed but undesirable.

Basenjis do not bark, only occasionally do they make a whining sound. To be able to follow them when tracking game the African hunters hang a wooden bell round their necks (2). Before going out to hunt the bell is plugged with grass so that the dogs won't start up the game prematurely.

1 ♂

Some tribes believe the bells have
a magic power which serves to protect
the dogs against attack by a leopard. In
the Sudan Basenjis are called 'leaping
dogs' because they often leap high up in
the tall grass in order to get their
bearings when pursuing game.

The Basset Hound was developed by crossing the French Basset and the Bloodhound. It first appeared at English dog shows in 1875 but originated in North America. British breeders, however, also contributed to its development mainly by adding the blood of the Basset Artésien-Normand, which lightened the build inherited from the Bloodhound. Not until 1883 was the Basset Hound reintroduced to North America. Originally the dogs of this breed were used as excellent trackers, nowadays they are kept almost exclusively as housedogs.

France is the native land of several breeds of bassets, short-legged hounds and zealous hunters. The Basset Bleu de Gascogne is perhaps the most elegant of all. This breed is derived from short-legged mutations of the Grand Bleu de Gascogne which were crossed with the Basset Artésien-Normand and the Petit Bleu de Gascogne. Despite its elegant appearance and excellent hunting qualities, this breed is only rarely kept.

Most bassets have a short, smooth coat and in that respect the Basset Griffon Vendéen differs markedly from the others for its coat is harder and longer, although it lies close to the body. There are two types: a heavier type suitable for hunting hares and larger game, like other bassets, and a lighter type used for hunting rabbits.

All bassets are independent and slightly stubborn dogs which require a firm hand.

Basset Hound (1)
Height: 33–38 kg. **Weight:** about 23 kg.
Colour: any recognised hound colour.
The distribution of the colour and markings is not important.

Basset Bleu de Gascogne (2)
Height: about 33 cm. **Weight:** about 15 kg. **Colour:** blue or white with black spots or mantle and with red markings on the cheeks, muzzle, inside of the ears and on the legs. The skin of this breed is black or white with black spots.

3

2 ♂

Basset Griffon Vendéen (3)
Height: larger type 38–42 cm, smaller
type 34–38 cm. **Weight:** larger type
18 kg, smaller type 15 kg. **Colour:**
self-coloured (yellow, brown,
whitish-grey), bicoloured (white and
orange, white and black, white and grey,
white and red), or tricoloured (white,
black and red; white, grey and red).

1 ♀

Beagle and Harrier

The breeding of dogs which ran in packs in pursuit of prey with riders on horseback at their heels dates from the days when the chase first became a popular pastime. Most of these dogs were bred to hunt deer and foxes. Equally popular, however, was the hunting of hares for which dogs of a smaller size were better suited. The smallest breed used as a hunting dog in packs is the Beagle. According to existing records, such dogs were already kept by Henry VII. The roots of the Beagle breed can be traced to dog packs dating from the middle of the eighteenth century when French hounds were brought to England. These were crossed with the Foxhound and French Basset Hound to obtain a breed with an extremely acute sense of smell and immense endurance, a breed which pursues game with loud barking.

The Beagle became very popular because it is a very peace-loving dog and is readily controlled even in a large pack. A friendly, affectionate and intelligent dog, it is also often kept as a house pet. Because of its disposition and physiological characteristic, in recent times the Beagle has, sadly, often been used for laboratory experiments. Today the Beagle is most widespread in the USA and France, where packs of these dogs may still be encountered at hare coursing.

For centuries Beagles of various sizes were raised together. Not until the twentieth century did the larger-sized Beagle begin to be bred separately, gradually developing into a separate breed called the Harrier.

2 ♂

Beagle
Height: 33–40 cm. **Weight:** not officially prescribed. **Colour:** solid liver or white with yellow, orange, red, blue or black patches, in any combination whatsoever, but always with a white-tipped tail. Liver and white is not acceptable. As a rule the dogs are tricoloured (1). Besides smooth-haired Beagles, a rough-haired variety is occasionally bred with a coat that is wiry and very dense.

Harrier
Height: 48–53 cm. **Weight:** about 25 kg.
Colour: white with patches of any colour from black to orange. Most common are dogs with intense liver patches on a white ground. Often encountered are dogs with a coloured mantle covering the whole of the back (2). The tip of the tail is always white.

1 ♀

These breeds belong to the group of dogs which follow their prey solely by scent and whose common characteristic is their pendulous ears. The Bloodhound is believed to be a descendant of the ancient Celtic hounds and probably also carries the blood of the Mastiff. Mention of these dogs is made as early as the seventh century, the best known dogs being those of St Hubert's Monastery in Ardennes, noted for its development of this breed; to this day one still often comes across the names Hubertushund, Chien de Saint Hubert, and the like. The English name Bloodhound, given to these dogs which came to England in 1066 with William the Conqueror, was supposed to indicate merely that they are noble dogs of pure blood. The Bloodhound has an extraordinarily acute sense of smell and is able to pursue even a very old scent (in some cases more than 48 hours old). For this reason it was used not only to hunt game but in sixteenth- and seventeenth-century England it also helped law enforcement officers to track down poachers and thieves.

The Bloodhound is a very peace-loving and good-natured dog, a good companion but a poor watchdog; it barks at intruders but otherwise takes no notice of them.

In the early seventeenth century Bloodhounds were taken to Virginia, England's first colony in North America. In the eighteenth century they were crossed there with Foxhounds and perhaps also with terriers to obtain a breed of dogs called Coonhounds, used especially for hunting racoons.

2 ♂

Bloodhound
Height: dog 63–69 cm, bitch 58–63 cm.
Weight: dog 41–50 kg, bitch 36–45 kg.
Colour: black and tan, red (1), ranging from beige to mahogany, liver and tan, or liver with a black mantle on the back, sides, upper neck and head. The skin of Bloodhounds is relatively thin, mainly on the head, where it forms typical loose folds on the cheeks and forehead. The lips form deep hanging flews overlapping the jaw by about 5 cm. The ears are very long, set low, and fall in graceful folds – they are equal in length to, or longer than, the muzzle. The skin on the ears is extremely thin. On the neck the skin forms a pronounced dewlap.

Coonhound (2)
Height: 58–68 cm. **Weight:** 25–35 kg.
Colour: black and tan.

1 ♀

Borzoi

The word *borzoi* is actually the Russian name for all greyhound breeds but worldwide it is applied only to this particular breed which was once very popular with the Russian aristocracy. Borzois were kept in packs, sometimes numbering more than 1,000 dogs. They were used for hunting hare, red deer, wild boar, foxes and wolves. The Borzoi's task was to overtake large game after it had been driven out of the woods into open country by a pack of hounds, and to hold the quarry in one place until the arrival of the huntsmen. As a rule three Borzois were sent out after a wolf. Guns were not used in hunting – the wolf, held at bay by the Borzois, was traditionally killed by a sportsman with a blow on the nose.

The late nineteenth century marked the onset of the greatest era in the breeding of the Borzoi. The person responsible for this was the Grand Duke Nikolai Nikolaievitch with his famed Perchino kennel in Tula. To this day dogs from this kennel influence the appearance and standard of the breed.

The first Borzoi was brought to England during the reign of Queen Victoria, as a gift to the Queen from Tsar Alexander II. The Borzois from English kennels, however, were smaller, of weaker build and less hairy than the famed dogs of the Russian kennels.

A typical pack hound, the Borzoi is a peaceful dog, does not fight or bite, is very quiet and barks very little. It is obedient, aloof, but wary, and very fierce in defending its owner. It is not often seen in races, but with good training it will attain a speed of about 50 km per hour.

Height: dog about 74 cm, bitch about 68 cm. The larger the better, but not at the expense of the dog's symmetry. **Weight:** 35–45 kg. **Colour:** usually solid white or white with yellow, orange, red (1, 2), brindle or grey patches, also self-coloured specimens in any of the aforesaid colours. Typical of darker-coloured dogs is a dark mask. Tan markings are allowed but are not desirable. In self-coloured dogs the head, breast, belly and lower part of the legs must be a lighter hue than the body. An interesting aspect in the behaviour of the Borzoi, one that differs from that of all other dogs, is the positioning of the ears. A Borzoi expresses his joy and friendliness by dropping his ears and folding them down on the head, which, in other dogs, always denotes a threatening attitude.

2

1

Dachshunds

Dachshunds are a very old breed of which written mention was made as early as the ninth and tenth centuries. Old German texts call it the Bibarhund, but in those days these dogs had ears that were carried erect. Many breeds participated in the development of the present type of Dachshund – scent hounds, pointers and pinschers, as well as terriers. The result was a short-legged dog suitable for underground work in burrows, particularly good in tracking and following a scent, and in working as a beater, slowly and with loud barking. The first standard was set up in 1879 and since then the Dachshund has become one of the most widespread breeds.

Dachshunds are of three types – smooth-haired (3), long-haired (1, 4) and wire-haired (2), each in two different sizes according to weight and possibly also chest measurement, namely Standard and Miniature. At shows the individual types, as well as sizes, are judged separately. The short-haired type is considered to be the oldest. The long-haired type perhaps includes certain spaniels in its ancestry, and the wire-haired type was developed by crossing the smooth-haired with terriers, mainly the Dandy Dinmont Terrier.

Dachshunds are very intelligent, independent, resourceful, occasionally self-willed, affectionate and undemanding. They are very good with children.

Height: 20–25 cm. **Weight:** Standard smooth-haired, dog up to 11.3 kg, bitch up to 10.4 kg; Standard long-haired 7.7–8.2 kg; Standard Wire-haired, dog 9–10 kg, bitch 8.2–9 kg. Chest measurement for Standard not officially prescribed. Miniature (all types) 4.5–5 kg. Chest measurement 35 cm. **Colour:** all colours are allowed except pure black and pure white without pigmentation. Solid colours are red (1), tan, russet (2), with or without brindle, or bicoloured – black (3), brown or grey with tan markings, or dappled. The nose and nails of black dogs should be black, in brown dogs preferably black or brown.

1

4

Foxhounds

In the early seventeenth century, the fashion in France, of hunting game with packs of hounds, also became a fashion in England. Horses as well as dogs bred for this purpose were often presented as gifts by the French King Henry IV to the English King James I. In England these dogs were further crossed with the Talbot (now extinct) and with dogs called Southern Hounds and Northern Hounds, according to the literature of that time. To obtain greater swiftness Greyhound blood was also added. The development of the dogs naturally differed according to the breeding choices of the owners of the various packs, but later the Foxhound type became uniform. In a pack these are excellent chasers but have an aversion to thickets and difficult terrain. For this reason Foxhound packs had to be accompanied, or rather supplemented, by various kinds of terriers which would drive out game seeking shelter in such impenetrable places or in holes.

The first Foxhounds were brought to North America in 1650. Later other dogs were imported – from England, Ireland and France – and crossing with these produced a type suitable for American conditions. The American Foxhound, however, has a very non-uniform breeding base and the owners of the individual packs do not show any particular interest in unifying the breed.

Foxhounds are happiest in a pack. They are not suitable as housedogs.

2 ♂

Foxhound
Height: 60–69 cm. **Weight:** about 35 kg.
Colour: black, tan or white in all combinations of the three or mixed colours. Tricolour dogs (1) either have vividly coloured patches or a dark mantle completely covering the back. Foxhound packs pursue game with loud barking. The combined barking should produce a chorus pleasant to the ear, and owners of such packs often look out for dogs with a voice of a specific pitch or inflection which is still lacking in their pack.

American Foxhound (2)
Height: 56–64 cm; bitches are slightly smaller than dogs. **Weight:** 30–35 kg.
Colour: any hound colour is permitted. The coat of the American Foxhound is slightly longer than that of the Foxhound. Unlike the latter the American Foxhound is sometimes also used as a tracker and scent hound.

1 ♀

143

Greyhound, Magyar Agár and Galgo Español

The Greyhound was brought to the British Isles a very long time ago, probably by the Celts in the fourth century BC. It was highly prized and not everyone was allowed to raise and keep this breed. Preserved to this day, for example, is the decree of Canute the Great, King of England and Denmark, dating from the years 1017–35, forbidding the keeping of the Greyhound by any except the nobility and landed gentry. The Greyhound was used in hunting, mostly for hares but also for red deer and possibly even wolves. The year 1561 marked the beginning of the era of dog races, which rapidly increased the popularity of the Greyhound. Without doubt it is the fastest of all dogs, attaining a speed of more than 60 km per hour. The Greyhound hunts primarily by sight. However, thanks to the blood of certain other breeds which took part in its development, it has a better nose than other greyhound or gazehound breeds and can even follow the trail of a hare which is lost from sight.

The Greyhound is not a dog for everybody. It requires a great deal of exercise, is rather distrustful and does not like children or cats.

The Greyhound influenced most of the greyhound/gazehound breeds found in Europe. In the ninth century gazehounds were brought to Europe by the Magyars. In the twelfth century Greyhound blood was added to increase the speed of the original dogs and to make them more graceful. The result was the breed called the Magyar Agár (Hungarian Greyhound) officially recognised by the FCI in 1966.

Gazehounds were brought to Spain by the Saracens where they were developed, also with the addition of Greyhound blood, into the breed called Galgo Español. This is the only Greyhound breed native to the western Mediterranean.

2 ♂

Greyhound (1)
Height: dog 71–76 cm, bitch 68–71 cm.
Weight: 20–25 kg. **Colour:** all colours; usually black, white, red, blue, yellow-brown, fawn, brindle, or any of the aforesaid colours with white.

Magyar Agár (2)
Height: 55–62 cm. **Weight:** 22–31 kg.
Colour: black, yellow, red, grey, brindle; it may also be patched with white and, exceptionally, solid white.

Galgo Español (3)
Height: 60–65 cm. **Weight:** 20–30 kg.
Colour: usually cinnamon, chestnut-brown, red, black, sandy (lion-colour), with or without white, or combinations of these colours.

3 ♂

1 ♂

145

Ibizan Hound, Portuguese Hound and Sicilian Hound

In the Mediterranean region there exists a whole group of hound breeds which greatly resemble dogs depicted on the walls of ancient Egyptian tombs. Presumably these dogs were brought from Africa to the European coast of the Mediterranean by the Phoenecians who had a brisk trade there.

The Ibizan Hound is native to the isles of Ibiza, Formentera, Mallorca and Minorca and to the coastal districts of Catalonia. It is used primarily for hunting hare, rabbit and feathered game, either singly or in small packs.

The very similar Portuguese Hound (Podenco Portugues) is found in Portugal in three sizes, the largest used for hunting larger game, the smallest for hunting hare and rabbit.

Both of the aforesaid breeds occur in three types with different coats — smooth-haired, long-haired, and rough-haired – the latter two lack an undercoat.

The Sicilian Hound (Cirneco dell' Etna) is an old breed descended from the ancient *canes sagaces*. It is found only in Sicily. It has remained very pure without any special measures being taken. Following the Second World War a group of enthusiasts took on the task of continuing to breed and develop this interesting and very ancient breed.

2 ♀

Ibizan Hound
Height: 56–74 cm. **Weight:** 19–23 kg.
Colour: white with red patches or mantle (1), white with lion-coloured markings, solid white, reddish-brown or lion colour.

Portuguese Hound
Height: large size 55–70 cm, medium size 50–55 cm, small size 20–30 cm.
Weight: according to size 25–30 kg, 15–20 kg, and 10 kg respectively. **Colour:** yellow, fawn (2), grey-black, either self-coloured or with white.

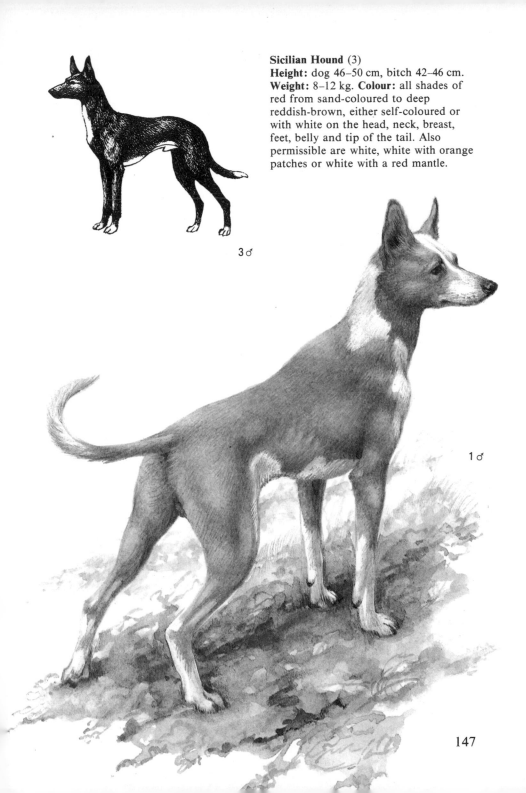

Sicilian Hound (3)
Height: dog 46–50 cm, bitch 42–46 cm.
Weight: 8–12 kg. **Colour:** all shades of
red from sand-coloured to deep
reddish-brown, either self-coloured or
with white on the head, neck, breast,
feet, belly and tip of the tail. Also
permissible are white, white with orange
patches or white with a red mantle.

3 ♂

1 ♂

147

Irish Wolfhound and Deerhound

According to the Irish Jesuit Edmund Ignatius Hogan, who devoted much time to the study of this breed, the first written mention of these dogs dates from the year 391, in an epistle in which the Roman Consul Quintus Aurelius Symmachus thanks his brother Flavianus for the Irish wolf hounds which attracted much interest in the Roman arena. The Irish Wolfhound breed was at the pinnacle of its popularity between the twelfth and sixteenth centuries, when large hunts were a favourite sport. The Wolfhound was also much sought after in other countries and was often exported. When wolves became extinct in the British Isles interest in these dogs began to wane and they became increasingly scarce, and in 1652 the Irish Parliament finally issued a law prohibiting the export of the Irish Wolfhound. For nearly 200 years the breed just barely held its own until 1862, when the English dog breeder Captain Graham took on the task of reviving it. By crossbreeding the remaining specimens of the practically extinct breed with the Deerhound and German Mastiff he established the present-day type, which received a standard in 1885.

A similar large dog of the greyhound family was developed also in Scotland, namely the Deerhound. The first depictions of these dogs are in Perthshire cave paintings dating from the period prior to the Christian era. It reached the height of its popularity in the seventeenth century when large deer hunts were commonly held in Scotland. The collapse of the clan systems after the flight of King James II of England, and the introduction of firearms, also jeopardised the existence of the Deerhound. Nevertheless, there remained a few enthusiasts who continued to breed it and have kept the Deerhound alive to this day.

Neither of the two breeds has any practical use as a working dog nowadays, but they are kept as peaceful, friendly housedogs. The Irish Wolfhound is very good with children.

2 ♂

Irish Wolfhound
Height: dog at least 79 cm, bitch at least 71 cm. Some dogs measure as much as 120 cm at the shoulders. **Weight:** 40.9–54.5 kg. **Colour:** wheaten, grey, red, white, black-fawn, brindle (1), usually with a dark mask.

148

1 ♀

Deerhound
Height: dog at least 76 cm, bitch at least
71 cm. **Weight:** 36.5–45.5 kg. **Colour:**
slate grey, grey with brindle (2), yellow,
reddish-yellow and reddish-grey with
a black mask and black ears.

The dense, rough coat of both breeds
requires no special attention apart from
brushing and occasional combing.

Italian Greyhound (Piccolo Levriero Italiano)

This is the smallest of the greyhound breeds. Although it is called Italian, it most certainly originated in north Africa where it was kept and bred since ancient times. It is said that Cleopatra owned these small greyhounds. They spread throughout the Mediterranean region in early medieval times, kept for chasing hares and as pets of patrician ladies. Thus there gradually developed two different types: a larger, working dog and a smaller, more graceful dog kept as a pet of the rich. King Charles I brought the breed from France to England and the Piccolo Levriero Italiano soon spread throughout Europe. Frederick the Great had a whole pack of these dogs at Potsdam and his example was followed by others of the nobility. This is one of the most frequently depicted breeds in early portraits of men and women of noble birth. The Italian Greyhound was developed in England to its present form.

Nowadays these dogs are no longer used for hunting hares, rats and mice, but with proper training and gentle handling even this sensitive, fine, small greyhound may be used for racing. It is mostly kept as a pet, making an intelligent and affectionate companion.

Height: 32–38 cm. **Weight:** according to type – either less than 4.5 kg or more than 4.5 kg. At shows a small dog in perfect condition is given preference over a larger dog, but a larger dog in perfect condition is preferable to a small dog with faults. **Colour:** solid black (2), slate-grey (3), or isabella in all shades (1); white on the breast and on the legs is acceptable but not desirable. Black and tan is not permissible. The coat is short and velvety, the skin fine and smooth. The nose is always black, the eyes dark brown. The toenails are lighter or darker depending on the colour of the coat. Typical of the Italian Greyhound is the way it moves. Its step is short and high, reminiscent of that of carriage horses or a sequence in classical dressage.

Otterhound: see p. 124.

1 ♂

151

In southern Africa, from northern Cape Province to the Zambezi River, the African peoples kept dogs which had a ridge of hair along the spine growing in the reverse direction to the rest of the coat. These dogs guarded herds and were so courageous that they even stood up to lions. The Boers, who were avid hunters, obtained these dogs from the Hottentots and used them to develop a breed that had the same characteristics but weighed more and had greater strength than the original type. Mastiffs, Greyhounds, and even terriers figured in its ancestry. The 'ridge', or 'pronk' as it was called by the Boers, remained a characteristic of the breed. In 1874 several of these dogs were taken by a missionary to Rhodesia (present-day Zimbabwe), where the breed was later widely bred. The first standard dates from 1902, when the breed was given the official name of Rhodesian Ridgeback.

The Rhodesian Ridgeback is an extremely fast, courageous attacker, but very friendly and devoted to its owner and its family. Its method of attacking is unique – it flings the whole weight of its body at its prey or foe, either knocking it to the ground or at least causing it to lose its balance. When it attacks as one of a pack, the Rhodesian Ridgeback enables the other dogs to bring down big game successfully, even a lion. Nowadays, when men hunt with modern weapons, the Rhodesian Ridgeback is used more often as a service and watchdog, or as a retriever of smaller game. The short, dense and close-lying coat is glossy; it must not be wavy or silky. It requires no special care. Despite its short coat the Rhodesian Ridgeback is hardy and stands up well to all kinds of weather. It also adapts readily to widely varied climates.

Height: dog 63–67 cm, bitch 61–66 cm. **Weight:** 29–33 kg. **Colour:** light to reddish wheaten (1); a small patch of white on the breast and toes is allowed. A darker (not black) muzzle and tip of the tail is in conformity with the standard, but there must not be a mask which extends over the eyes.

A typical characteristic is the ridge of hair growing in the reverse direction beginning with two whorls, or crowns, behind the shoulder, which must be placed symmetrically and must extend to not more than one-third of the length of the ridge (2). The ridge is about 5 cm wide and gradually tapers towards the

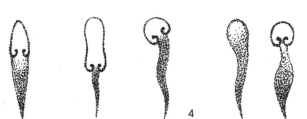

4

hind-quarters. It should begin
immediately behind the shoulders and
end at the line joining the haunches (3).
Incorrect shapes of whorls are shown
in Fig. 4.

2

3

1 ♂

Scent hounds are a very old group of dogs. Originally they followed the trail of the quarry and led the hunter to the game; after guns were invented they specialised in following the trail of wounded game, mainly through traces of blood. In the Bavarian Alps a lighter type of scent hound – the Bavarian Schweisshund – was developed for hunting chamois in the difficult terrain of those parts. It carries traces of hound blood and Hanoverian Schweisshund blood. The Hanoverian Schweisshund is descended from various types of dogs used as trackers at princely estates in Germany in the eighteenth century.

Scent hounds are used only for tracking game such as deer and that is why nowadays their use and distribution is restricted only to those regions where an abundance of deer makes keeping such dogs worth while, for their training takes several years and requires great patience and perseverance. Well-trained Schweisshunds, however, are capable of following a trail more than 24 hours old over a distance of many kilometres. Generally these hounds work on a leash. If they work freely without a leash they are either trained to return to their master and let him know, by means of an established signal, that they have found the quarry, or else they are trained to remain beside the quarry, barking continuously until their master arrives at the spot. In the latter instance, if the game is merely wounded the dog must hold the quarry until its master's arrival.

2 ♂

Bavarian Schweisshund
Height: 45–50 cm. **Weight:** about 25 kg.
Colour: dark red, reddish-brown, reddish-yellow (1), ochre, fawn to wheaten, grey-brown, brindle always with a darker back and with a dark mask.

Hanoverian Schweisshund
Height: 50–60 cm. **Weight:** 25–30 kg.
Colour: dark to light red, reddish-brown (2), usually with brindle, also grey-brown, or brown with black markings. There is a more or less distinct dark mask on the head and ears and sometimes a dark stripe running along the back.

3

When working on a leash Schweisshunds wear a broad collar with a swivel to which the long leash is attached. In order that the leash may be shortened and lengthened, it is coiled in a traditional way (3).

1 ♂

Since ancient times the peoples of Asia and north Africa used greyhound breeds for hunting in the steppes and semi-deserts. In time these developed into a number of types of dog, differing in size and coat, which can be divided into characteristic breeds. Naturally even within each breed one will find varied types depending on their place of origin and use.

North Africa and the Sinai Peninsula are the home of the breed known as the Sloughi. The Arabs devoted great attention to training these dogs. In their first year they hunted hare, at the age of two gazelles, and at the age of three large species of antelope. In the late nineteenth century the Sloughi appeared in Europe, first of all in the Netherlands and France.

As of 1981, the FCI recognised the greyhound of the Tuaregs, called the Azawakh after the oasis Asauak, as an independent breed. Until that time it had not been differentiated from the Sloughi.

The Middle East region, from Turkey through Syria to Iran and Saudi Arabia, is the home of the Saluki. It was and continues to be used for hunting hares, gazelles and jackals. On long trips the Saluki rides on the saddle of the horse or camel in front of its owner and only when the game is sighted does it spring down on command to chase the quarry until it wears it out. The Saluki came to Europe at the beginning of the nineteenth century when it was also brought to England. The first Saluki took part in races in the year 1927; two of the six that were at the starting line won the race, thus marking the beginning of the breed's spread in Europe.

2 ♂

Sloughi (1)
Height: 60–70 cm; ideal height for the dog is 68 cm, for the bitch 65 cm.
Weight: about 30 kg. **Colour:** sandy or yellow-red in all shades, with or without a dark mask, sometimes with a darker mantle.

Saluki (2)
Height: dog 58–71 cm, bitch 54–66 cm.
Weight: 14–25 kg. **Colour:** white, cream, fawn (2), grizzle, golden-red, golden-yellow, grey, black and tan, black with yellow markings, or a combination of the aforesaid colours.

Azawakh

Height: about 70 cm. **Weight:** about 30 kg. **Colour:** sandy, yellow-red to red, with a black mask. Sometimes there are brindled specimens, often with white markings on the head, breast and tip of the tail. The Azawakh (3) differs from the Sloughi (4) mainly in body format, line of the back, and several other, smaller details.

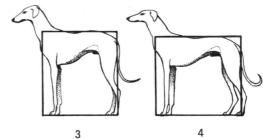

3   4

1 ♀

157

Spitzes are an old German breed known from as far back as the fifteenth century. The ancestors of these dogs, however, must be looked for amongst the dogs of later Stone Age dwellings. Different kinds of Spitz were kept and bred in various parts of Germany: in Württemberg mostly black, in Pomerania white, in Westphalia brown. Small Spitzes were raised mainly round Stutgart and in the lower Neckar River region, large Spitzes in the north. The Dutch have a large grey Spitz they call the Keeshond. The FCI, however, considers this breed to be the same as the German Wolf Spitz. In 1899 Spitz breeders in Germany joined ranks in the 'Verein für deutsche Spitze' (German Spitz Society) and set up standards for the various sizes and types of colouring of this breed.

Spitzes were bred primarily as watchdogs. Not only are they naturally vigilant and distrustful of strangers, but they have a further advantage in that they do not leave their post. They are undemanding, faithful and very handsome, and thus have all the prerequisites for becoming popular companion dogs as well. The original colours were augmented by further striking ones (e. g. orange) and the dogs' coats became more profuse and more attractive. Most popular nowadays are the Small Spitzes, which are more suitable as housedogs. These were bred in England from Spitzes brought there from Pomerania and acquired the name Pomeranian, which they have retained to this day.

Spitzes are divided, according to size, into several categories. In **height** the Wolf Spitz (1) measures at least 45 cm, the Great German Spitz (2) measures at least 40 cm, the Small Spitz (Pomeranian) (3) measures a maximum of 28 cm, and the Toy Spitz (4) measures a maximum of 22 cm. The Wolf Spitz differs from the Great German Spitz by having a more robust body and a coarser coat. The **weight** of the Wolf Spitz is about 30 kg; the Small Spitz may weigh a maximum of 2.5 kg; the weights of the Great German Spitz and Toy Spitz are not officially prescribed.

Colouring: wolf-grey, silvery grey with black-tipped hairs (1); white, without a yellow tinge; brown, the same dark brown all over; black, including the undercoat and skin; orange, the same solid colour all over (only in the Small Spitz – 5). The Small Spitz has been developed in other colours as well.

5

1

The Whippet was developed in northern England as a very fast greyhound breed for racing. Initially this dog was used in rabbit coursing, in which two Whippets competed in chasing a wild rabbit released into an arena. When this sport was prohibited in 1911, Whippets competed on a race track in chasing a scrap of cloth. The first rag racing meet was held as early as 1876. Nowadays Whippets primarily compete in chasing the mechanically propelled figure of a hare and the race is begun from starting boxes.

To this day the breed exhibits a slight non-uniformity because its development dates from as late as 1835–55 and included the participation of a number of breeds. Its forebears definitely include the Greyhound, but in great part also Italian Greyhounds and certain terriers. Thanks to these breeds, Whippets are extremely fast dogs on short tracks.

The Whippet is not merely a racing dog but also one of the most pleasant of household pets, providing it is given sufficient exercise. It is very clean, scrupulously avoiding puddles, mud and other dirt when out on a walk, affectionate, obedient and always good-natured. Whippets are fond of sun and warmth and perhaps that is why they are thought to be delicate. A hardy Whippet, which has been trained to tougher conditions from puppyhood, however, is not afraid of cold and does not even mind snow as long as it is not wet.

2

Height: dog 47–51 cm, bitch 44–47 cm. **Weight:** 7.5–12 kg. **Colour:** any solid colour or combination of colours. Whippets have typical thin rose ears (2).

The original coat is fine, short and as close-lying as possible. Besides this short-haired form (1) there are also wire-haired Whippets with a hard, wiry coat and dense undercoat. These, however, have not become very popular. In 1937 the American Whippet breeder Walter A. Wheeler began the purposeful selective breeding of long-haired Whippets with a coat resembling the Borzoi's. They also differ slightly in type, having a more arched back than other Whippets. They were exhibited at a show for the first time in 1981.

1 ♂

GUNDOGS

American Cocker Spaniel

In late nineteenth-century Britain spaniels were differentiated according to size. At that time the only spaniel bred in America was the so-called English Spaniel, a combination of Cocker Spaniel and Springer Spaniel. Its further development focused on emphasising certain external characteristics so that the outcome was a dog so different from the English Cocker Spaniel that it could no longer be considered as belonging to the same breed. In 1943 the American Cocker Spaniel was officially recognised as a separate breed with its own standard. The American Cocker Spaniel differs from the English Cocker Spaniel primarily in the shape of the head, its more profuse, slightly wavy coat, size, and more thickset body. It has the same temperament.

Originally the American Cocker Spaniel was also a hunting dog but was increasingly kept and bred only as a pet and is now usually a companion dog. Its profuse coat is readily soiled when working in the field and requires more care than that of the English Cocker Spaniel. Light stripping is also used in grooming. The American Cocker Spaniel must be combed and brushed at least once a day.

Height: dog 36.25–38.75 cm, bitch 33.75–36.25 cm. **Weight:** 10–12 kg. **Colour:** the same as for the English Cocker Spaniel. In self-coloured dogs (1) white marks are permitted on the chest and throat; the presence of white on other parts of the body is reason for disqualification. The feathering on the legs should not be lighter than the hair on the body.

1

The head of the American Cocker
Spaniel (2) is shorter and broader than
the head of the English Cocker Spaniel
(3), the skull is rounded, the brow
projecting and the jaws shorter. The
body is more robust, the legs shorter
and the chest deeper and broader. The
coat is silky, straight or only slightly
wavy, short on the head, medium long
on the body, ears, breast and belly, and
long and springy on the legs.

163

The Clumber Spaniel is apparently one of the oldest breeds of spaniels. It is said to have originated in France at the estate of the Duc de Noailles by the crossing of an old, now extinct type of spaniel and a French Basset Hound. At the time of the French Revolution, the Duc took his dogs to England, to the Duke of Newcastle's seat at Clumber Park. He himself returned to France where he died. The Duke of Newcastle continued to breed these excellent hunting dogs which, although slower, were more systematic and more reliable than other spaniels, and, unlike the latter, went about their work without giving tongue. The Clumber Spaniel is the heaviest of the spaniel breeds, but nevertheless it does not appear to be cumbersome. It is an excellent retriever and is especially popular for hunting feathered game because it puts up the game within short range of the sportsman's shotgun. Their calm, slow manner of working makes Clumbers great favourites for hunting in game-rich preserves where they cause a minimum of disturbance.

In the mid-nineteenth century, at Rosehill Park in Sussex, there originated a breed which definitely carries the blood of the Clumber Spaniel. The Sussex Spaniel has always been used exclusively as a working dog. Its typical characteristic is perseverance in hunting game, giving tongue all the while, which indicates that it carries the blood not only of spaniels but of other breeds as well. The Sussex Spaniel's appearance at shows came at a very late date and it never became very widespread. Even in England it is one of the least known breeds.

Clumber Spaniel (1)
Height: 42.5–45 cm. **Weight:** dog 34 kg, bitch 29.5 kg. **Colour:** white with lemon yellow patches; orange patches are permitted but are not desirable. All-white dogs with slight yellow markings on the head and fore-muzzle are preferred. The nose should be as dark as possible, best of all black, the eyes the darkest possible brown. The tail is held in line with the back.

Sussex Spaniel (2)
Height: 38–41 cm. **Weight:** about 22 kg. **Colour:** golden-yellow with lighter-tipped hairs; dark reddish-brown is not allowed. The nose is reddish-brown, the eyes hazel. The tail is set low and never held above the line of the back.

1

The English Cocker Spaniel is one of the oldest original breeds of hunting dogs. Originally spaniels were considered to be a uniform group of hunting dogs and were differentiated only according to weight — weighing less than 11 kg and more than 11 kg. The larger dogs were called Springing Spaniels, the smaller Cocking Spaniels. And it was from the smaller type, used mainly for hunting woodcock, that the Cocker Spaniel was developed. The name appeared for the first time in 1893 and the year 1902 marked the establishment of the first standard for this breed, which has remained practically unchanged to the present day.

The hunting capabilities of the Cocker Spaniel are outstanding: it has an excellent nose, is a willing tracker, gives loud tongue when putting up game and is a good retriever. It is very easily trained and readily controlled, affectionate towards members of the household but suspicious and wary of strangers. It is therefore not surprising that it also became popular outside the realm of the hunt. However, the wave of fashion which brought the Cocker Spaniel to the pinnacle of its popularity in some countries did not benefit the breed because quantity became more important than quality, in terms of both disposition and appearance. This trend did not, fortunately, substantially affect the innate hunting qualities of the Cocker Spaniel; there always remained plenty of kennels where Cocker Spaniels were trained solely as working dogs for hunting.

The long, close-lying, silky coat of the Cocker Spaniel requires daily brushing and combing and for show purposes will need 'hairdressing'.

2

Height: 38–41 cm. **Weight:** 12.7–14.5 kg. **Colour:** very diverse – either solid black, red or gold (2), or multicoloured, i.e. white with black, red or orange patches or small splashes, or blue roans. Dogs are described as tricoloured (1) if they have tan markings on the head and legs in addition to patches in one of the aforesaid colours. Roans may also be tricoloured. Black and tan gives a black ground colour with tan markings on the head, inside the ears, legs and feet, tan feathering and a tan patch round the anus. This type of colouring is judged in the group of self-coloured Cocker Spaniels. The tail of the Cocker Spaniel should be docked but not too short. It is held in line with the back, never upright.

1 ♂

The lower it is held, the better. The
position of the ears is also important –
they should be set on low, level with the
outer corner of the eye.

Setters acquired their name because of their method of indicating the presence of game – they crouch – and were at one time called 'sitting dogs'. All setters are typical British breeds of long-haired gundogs but their ancestors must be looked for elsewhere, amongst the Spanish pointers (Perdigueros) and French spaniels (Epagneuls). Setter breeds originated in the seventeenth century. The oldest is the English Setter. It is also the swiftest and most zealous. Responsible for its development was Sir Edward Laverack, who, around 1825, began selective interbreeding of dogs with good hunting qualities. Laverack's setters had a perfect external appearance but were very self-willed and hard to control. That is why another English breeder, R. Purcell Llewellin, crossed Laverack setters with Irish Setters (2) and Gordon Setters (3), which had a more equable disposition. Most present-day English Setters are descended from this stock.

A special breed of setter originated in Ireland. Its forebears include the French Epagneuls and Irish Pointers. Up until the end of the eighteenth century these dogs were coloured red and white. Litters, however, occasionally included solid red pups which were popular for reasons of fashion and from these was gradually developed the present-day Irish Setter, coloured a rich mahogany red.

The English Setter's speciality is searching for game in open country and it has little talent for tracking and retrieving. However, it may be taught to do even this with consistent training. The Irish Setter has a strong hunting instinct, which makes young dogs harder to control. However, it possesses an inherent willingness for retrieving and water work and is thus more readily trained as a multipurpose gundog.

3

English Setter
Height: dog 65–68 cm, bitch 61–65 cm.
Weight: dog 27–30 kg, bitch 25.5–30 kg.
Colour: white with black (1), white with yellow, white with liver, or tricolour, i.e. white with black and tan. Small patches are preferred to large patches.

1 ♀

Irish Setter (2)
Height: about 55 cm. **Weight:** 26–29 kg.
Colour: solid mahogany red.

English Springer Spaniel
and Welsh Springer Spaniel

The Springer Spaniel was developed from a larger type of old English spaniel. Its name is derived from the manner in which it puts up game. It flushes feathered game which it has found, by a series of several short leaps. It also has another typical characteristic which distinguishes it from other spaniels – when walking the forelegs move straight forward from the shoulders so that the feet reach far to the front; in other words its gait is somewhat like that of a horse. This is very striking especially at a slow pace. Other spaniels tend to trot, taking small steps.

The English Springer Spaniel is a breed with excellent hunting qualities. Its relatively large build gives it greater endurance than other spaniels and enables it to carry bigger game. The stud book of this breed goes back to 1813, but the standard was not set until 1902.

Kept and bred in Wales, mainly in the Neath Valley, is a breed of spaniels descended from the Epagneul Breton. These dogs were brought to Wales from Brittany by the Gauls and were further developed there. In 1912 the breed received its own standard and was given the name Welsh Springer Spaniel. It is a dog with extraordinarily well-developed hunting capabilities.

English Springer Spaniel
Height: 50–51 cm. **Weight:** 22.7 kg.
Colour: liver and white, black and white
(1) or one of these combinations with
tan markings.

Welsh Springer Spaniel (2)
Height: 46–48 cm. **Weight:** 16–21 kg.
Colour: only white with rich red patches
is allowed. The coat should have a silky
lustre.

170

Authorities often argue about the origin of the name spaniel, or *épagneul*. According to some breeders it is derived from the Carthaginian word *span*, meaning wild rabbit, which was hunted by these dogs. According to others it is derived from the old Celtic word *espana*, currently used in the Basque language, designating the boundary hedges which often sheltered game which the dogs started up. According to a third group of authorities the name *épagneul* is derived from the Basque word *epantar*, which they translate as 'starting up'.

1

2

171

French Epagneuls are a group of breeds which participated in the development of many present-day breeds of gundogs and trackers. They carry the blood of Arabian dogs brought to France from north Africa at some time in the distant past. The hybrid offspring of these greyhound-like dogs and long-haired hounds were called *chiens couchant,* hence they were probably used as gundogs. In Brittany the breed was also influenced by Springer Spaniels brought there from England by the Celts. Later on the Epagneuls Bretons were further crossed with setters and selective breeding also fixed what had been a chance aberration — the rudimentary tail. The Epagneul Breton is the only spaniel which points, apparently due to the setter blood in its veins.

The Epagneul Français is an older breed of French spaniel. It was one of the most popular breeds in the seventeenth and eighteenth centuries and is shown in most of the sporting portraits of that time. Later, however, it fell into oblivion and in the nineteenth century was on the verge of extinction until, thanks to the patient efforts of enthusiastic dog breeders, this readily trained dog was re-established and regained its popularity.

Developed for work in the marshes of northern France was the very similar Epagneul Picard, which differs by having a squarer outline and a rougher coat. It is very easily controlled but does not tolerate a heavy hand.

All Spaniels are hunting dogs which work within a relatively short range (within the range of a shotgun). They chase quarry out of dense thickets and retrieve wounded game.

2 ♂

3 ♀

Epagneul Breton
Height: 46–51 cm. **Weight:** 13–15 kg.
Colour: permitted by the standard are white with chestnut-brown patches (1), white with orange patches, or grey-roan with one of the aforesaid colours.

Epagneul Français (2)
Height: 54–65 cm. **Weight:** 25–30 kg.
Colour: white with chestnut-brown patches, with white predominating and the patches not too large.

1

Epagneul Picard (3)
Height: 55–60 cm. **Weight:** about 25 kg.
Colour: grey with chestnut-brown
patches, mainly at the root of the tail;
often with red patches on the head and
legs.

The German Short-haired Pointer is without doubt the most widespread breed of pointer in Europe and it is often encountered also in other continents. The original type, known as far back as the seventeenth century, was much heavier and more robust than the present-day breed. It was a reliable gundog but a slow and shorter-distance worker and could not compete with the English gundogs which began to arrive in Europe in the mid-nineteenth century. In 1890, however, a number of dog breeders in Germany founded the 'Klub Kurzhaar' (Short-haired Pointer Club) and, using English Pointers to improve the original type, developed dogs of outstanding qualities which inherited from the original German gundogs a willingness to track game, retrieve and work in water, and from the Pointers a keener nose, swiftness and steady pointing. This makes the German Short-haired Pointer a truly versatile hunting dog.

The qualities of the German Long-haired Pointer make it popular for work in woods. Its perseverance in searching out and tracking game, its inherent keenness and slower method of work along with greater hardiness have made it a favourite, primarily with professional foresters and gamekeepers. Because it is naturally suspicious of strangers, it is also an excellent watchdog. The standard for this breed, established in 1879, has remained practically unchanged to this day.

A third German Pointer is the German Wire-haired Pointer which is an excellent retriever, good on land and in water.

2 ♀

German Short-haired Pointer
Height: dog 58–64 cm, bitch 53–59 cm.
Weight: dog 25–32 kg, bitch 20.5–27 kg.
Colour: liver, self-coloured or with white markings on the breast and legs, white with liver patches or spots (1), always with a liver head. The same variations also with black.

German Long-haired Pointer
Height: 61–63.5 cm. **Weight:** about 30 kg. **Colour:** brown (2) or brown and white with brown patches or spots. The coat is about 3–5 cm long on the back and sides, shorter on the head. It is longer on the front of the neck, breast, belly and toes and forms feathers on the legs and on the tail. Sometimes the tail is slightly shortened by docking.

German Wire-haired Pointer
Height: dog 60–67 cm, bitch 56–62 cm.
Weight: dog 25–34 kg, bitch 20.5–29 kg.
Colour: liver and white, solid liver,
black and white. The outer coat is thick
and harsh and the undercoat is dense.
The coat lies close to the body.

1 ♀

In eighteenth-century Germany dogs called Hühnerhunde, or Wachtelhunde, were used for hunting feathered game. They were used in falconry as well as for flushing quarry of all kinds from thickets and reedbeds. Later these trackers became less popular and were threatend with extinction. In the late nineteenth century the German breeder Friedrich Roberth founded the 'Deutscher Wachtelhundklub' (German Spaniel Club). Together with other enthusiasts, particularly Dr. Steffens and a forester named Friesse, he gathered the remaining purebred dogs and set about regenerating the breed. Despite the keen competition of hunting spaniels the Deutscher Wachtelhund won favour because of its outstanding qualities, especially with professional foresters.

A similar breed of tracker, the Wetterhund, is used in Friesland in the Netherlands. It was bred for work in water and, being keen enough to attack even otters, was also used by huntsmen for this purpose. Typical of this dog are the long hairs at the base of the ears and the tail curled in a spiral. The coat is curly and oily. Nowadays this breed is no longer used for hunting in Friesland but kept instead as a watchdog. It has retained its hunting qualities, however, and farmers often use it to catch moles.

2 ♂

German Spaniel
Height: 45–52 cm. **Weight:** about 25 kg.
Colour: brown, often with white markings on the breast and toes, also white with brown patches or markings (1). Other colours are not desirable. The muzzle as well as the eyes is brown. The coat is dense, glossy and wavy, and is curly on the neck, nape and ears. The legs and tail are feathered. There should be as little hair as possible between the toes. There are often elongated hairs on both sides of the chest (called a *jabot*). An important characteristic of the breed is the flat head with a practically undiscernable stop. Under no circumstances should the head resemble that of a spaniel.

Wetterhund
Height: dog 50—55 cm, bitch 48—53 cm. **Weight:** about 35 kg. **Colour:** black, brown or blue-roan, also black or brown patches on a white ground (2).

1

This breed of retriever probably originated in the mid-nineteenth century. The most likely theory of its origin is the one according to which the Golden Retriever's forebears include Russian, in all probability Caucasian, shepherd dogs. The degree to which other breeds, e.g. Bloodhounds and setters, participated in its development is not precisely known. Be this as it may, the result is an active retriever with great endurance, an excellent nose and great enthusiasm for water work. It is good with children and is thus often kept as a friendly, attractive household pet. However, it requires plenty of exercise. Its handsome, long, smooth or slightly wavy coat, with its dense, waterproof undercoat, needs a fair amount of care, i.e. daily brushing, and combing several times a week. It is popular not only in England but in many other countries as well.

The Flat-coated Retriever is another retriever with a rather long coat, which developed at the same period. It carries traces of the blood of dogs brought to England from Newfoundland and also of setters. It has excellent hunting qualities and has also proved to be an excellent companion dog, being particularly fond of children. Before the First World War it was one of the most popular dogs in England. Later, however, it was ousted by the Labrador Retriever and Golden Retriever. Only nowadays is it beginning to regain its popularity.

The work of retrievers differs somewhat from that of other hunting dogs. The retriever accompanies the huntsman, follows the scent and brings in the killed or wounded game on command.

2 ♀

Golden Retriever (1)
Height: dog 56–61 cm, bitch 45–56 cm.
Weight: dog 32–37 kg, bitch 27–32 kg.
Colour: any shade of gold or cream, but there must be no tinge of red or mahogany. Single white hairs on the chest are permissible.

Flat-coated Retriever
Height: dog 58-61 cm, bitch 56–59 cm.
Weight: 25–34 kg. **Colour:** black (2) or liver. The Flat-coated Retriever differs from the Labrador Retriever in its height and the character of its coat, which is fine, dense and lies close to the body with the primary hairs longer and glossier than the undercoat. The coat is thickest on the forelegs, thighs and tail.

1

Various setters were bred at Gordon Castle in Banffshire as early as 1770 or thereabouts. Later, however, the kennel was closed. Around 1835, the Duke of Richmond and Gordon revived the fame of the kennel and set himself the goal of developing a setter that would be heavier, hardier and keener than other setters. It is known that he used a Collie bitch, the Bloodhound, the Irish Setter and probably also the Pointer. He created a large breeding base and acquired many patrons interested in his dogs. The standard was established in 1927, the year the British Gordon Setter Club was founded.

The Gordon Setter is less swift than other setters but, unlike them, can work with a low nose and can therefore be put to good use as a scent hound and tracker. As a rule it is a better, more reliable retriever, as well as excellent at working in water. In other words, of all the setters it has the best developed talents for multipurpose work – it can be used in fields and water as well as in woods, is a willing retriever and a good tracker.

Because of its handsome appearance it is often kept as a housedog. It has an affectionate, happy disposition and is good with children, but suspicious of strangers.

Height: dog 66 cm, bitch 62 cm. **Weight:** 25.5–29.5 kg. **Colour:** shining coal-black with rich tan markings (1). The markings consist of two small tan patches above the eyes, tan edging of the mouth which must not extend beyond the base of the muzzle, two tan patches on the front of the chest, tan colouring on the back of the hind legs and thighs reaching to the outer side at the knee and on down to the toes. On the forelegs tan colouring on the back extends from the elbow to the toes, and on the front from the toes

3

2

1

to the pastern joint. There is also a tan
patch round the anus.

Compared to the Irish (2) and English
Setters, the Gordon Setter (3) has
a broader skull with the part from
occiput to stop longer than the face
(from stop to nose).

The Hungarian plains between the Danube and Tisa rivers were always rich in small game, mainly partridges, hares and, as of the eighteenth century, pheasants, and so it is not surprising that several breeds of hunting dogs originated here. Most important of these is the Hungarian Vizsla, an excellent and versatile pointer. Similar dogs were first recorded in the eighteenth century at the Zayngroc estate. Their forebears may have included yellow hunting dogs brought to Europe by the Turks. They also carry the blood of the German Short-haired Pointer, the Hanoverian Schweisshund and several breeds of hounds. In 1917 Kaposvar became the main breeding centre and that year also marks the beginning of pure breeding.

The Hungarian Vizsla is a readily controlled and easily trained dog, an enthusiastic retriever and a good tracker, and some individuals are also excellent at working in water. Because of these outstanding qualities and undoubtedly also because of its handsome, unusual colouring, this breed is popular not only in Hungary but in many other countries. Compared with other gundogs it takes longer to mature and certain inherent traits, such as pointing, take time to become established.

Height: dog 57–64 cm, bitch 53–60 cm. **Weight:** 20–30 kg. **Colour:** russet gold (1). Brownish or pale yellow are not permitted by the standard. The coat is short, straight and coarse, oily and springy to the touch. The pigmentation on the entire body is a rich yellow-brown. The nose, rims of the eyelids, pads on the feet and nails are the same colour but slightly darker; they should never be black. The tail is usually docked. A typical characteristic of the breed is a brisk, long stride. When searching for game it usually does so at a lengthy gallop, but remaining in constant contact with its master by working within a relatively short range.

2

1

Hungarian Vizsla litters occasionally include pups with longer hair. In the 1930s Hungarian breeders developed the Rough-haired Hungarian Vizsla (2) by crossing these pups with the German Wire-haired Pointer. The coat of this rough-haired pointer is 3–4 cm long, hard and without a gloss. It provides more protection against cold and against icy water when the dogs are used to hunt and retrieve ducks. The colour is the same as for the Short-haired Hungarian Vizsla. The breed is not fully stabilised as yet, and now and then litters contain pups with unsuitable coats or colouring.

Very little is known about the origin of the Irish Water Spaniel. According to some authorities its forebears included the Poodle and the Irish Setter. Its character tends to support this theory because the Irish Water Spaniel is responsive to training and is an eager worker like the Poodle, and has an excellent nose like the Irish Setter. It also probably carries traces of spaniel blood as well, because it is an enthusiastic tracker. The breed is certainly very old, as indicated by the absolutely true breeding of the Irish Water Spaniel, without any infusion of the blood of other breeds.

The Irish Water Spaniel was first shown at Birmingham in 1862, when it was recognised as a separate breed. It became very popular because of its excellent performance in hunting over very difficult terrain, where it demonstrated all its outstanding qualities. In also makes a very good companion dog for those who can provide it with plenty of exercise.

Irish Water Spaniels were taken to America and crossed with Curly-coated Retrievers to develop dogs which were suitable for American conditions of working in water, reeds and woodland thickets. The American Water Spaniel, also sometimes called the Boykin Spaniel, was officially recognised as a separate breed in 1940. It is exclusively a working dog and is not suitable as a housedog.

2 ♂

Irish Water Spaniel (1)
Height: dog 53–58 cm, bitch 51–56 cm.
Weight: 22–28 kg. **Colour:** rich dark liver, sometimes called puce-liver. White marks of any kind and white-tipped hairs are causes for eliminating the dog from further breeding. The coat is dense, curly, without an undercoat, longer on the belly and shorter on the neck than on the body. It should be oily and often has a purplish lustre. The hind legs should be covered with tassels, curled all the way down to the feet. About 7–10 cm of the tail is covered with close curls from the root, the remainder is covered with extremely short hair.

1

American Water Spaniel (2)
Height: 38–46 cm. **Weight:** 12–22 kg.
Colour: liver or chocolate. Small white
marks on the breast and toes are
permissible. It differs from the Irish
Water Spaniel at first glance not only by
its size but also by having the top of the
head flatter, with smooth hair and
a slight stop.

Labrador Retriever, Chesapeake Bay Retriever and Curly-coated Retriever

As far back as the seventeenth century Newfoundland seamen used large black dogs trained to swim between the shore and boats carrying various things. These water dogs were the forebears of the Newfoundland and Landseer as well as several other breeds. From the dogs that were brought to England from Newfoundland in the early nineteenth century, the third Earl of Malmesbury developed a breed of retrievers to which he gave the name Labrador Retriever. In the process he used Pointers, which gave the breed an excellent nose. This and the dog's extraordinary eagerness to retrieve are qualities that tie in excellently with the work of a far-ranging and steadfast Pointer in finding and retrieving game. The Labrador Retriever soon became the most popular of the retriever breeds. Because of its other good qualities, however, it also found employment as a guide dog for the blind and even as a police dog used in searching for narcotics.

History states that in 1807, when a British ship was wrecked off the coast of Maryland, two dogs were saved along with the crew. These were raised by a sportsman who discovered their good hunting qualities. Later crossings of these dogs with other imported breeds, such as the Irish Water Spaniel and Otterhound, gave rise to the American breed of retrievers called the Chesapeake Bay Retriever.

The youngest breed of retrievers is the Curly-coated Retriever, developed in England at the beginning of the present century and carrying the blood of the Labrador Retriever, Irish Water Spaniel, Poodle and various setters.

2 ♂

3 ♂

Labrador Retriever
Height: dog 56–57 cm, bitch 54–56 cm.
Weight: 25–30 kg. **Colour:** black (1), yellow or chocolate. The short coat is hard to the touch.

Chesapeake Bay Retriever (2)
Height: dog 58–66 cm, bitch 53–61 cm.
Weight: 27–32 kg. **Colour:** any shade of brown to yellow, self-coloured. A white mark on the chest and on the toes is permitted. The coat is short and thick, never longer than 3 cm. Dogs should have yellow eyes.

1 ♂

Curly-coated Retriever
Height: 63–69 cm. **Weight:** 31–36 kg.
Colour: black (3) or liver. Except for the
face and the skull, the coat forms thick,
short, hard curls all over, including the
ears and tail.

187

Large Münsterländer, Small Münsterländer and Drentse Patrijshond

Bred in Lower Saxony and the neighbouring part of the Netherlands were long-haired dogs used both for herding and hunting. At the beginning of the present century three breeds were developed, all closely related.

The Large (Grosser) Münsterländer was probably the least widespread. Despite its good hunting qualities it was superseded by other hunting dogs. It is only rarely encountered nowadays, and then generally only as a calm and affectionate companion dog.

The Small (Kleiner) Münsterländer is the smallest of the gundog breeds. A versatile dog, it combines the qualities of trackers, pointers and retrievers. If steady pointing is desired of the dog, however, it must be properly trained in this before being allowed to track and flush game. Its small size and gentle disposition make it a good housedog. It has become increasingly popular in recent years, mainly in France, Sweden and Norway.

The Drentse Patrijshond was bred from the same forebears as the first two breeds but in the Netherlands, where it was kept and used mainly by farmers for hunting partridges. It is perhaps the oldest of the three breeds because similar dogs appear in paintings which are several centuries old. It is a dog of good hunting qualities, gentle and good with children.

Large Münsterländer
Height: 58–62 cm. **Weight:** about 20 kg.
Colour: white with black patches (1) or smaller patches, also black roan. The tail is usually docked by two or three vertebrae.

3

Small Münsterländer
Height: dog 48–56 cm, bitch 44–52 cm.
Weight: about 16 kg. **Colour:** white with
brown patches or mantle (2), also brown
roan. The head is brown, sometimes
with a white blaze. The feathering on at
least the last third of the tail must be
white or white with spots. Pups are born
white with brown patches and only after
six to eight weeks do the typical brown
markings appear in the white coat.

Drentse Patrijshond (3)
Height: 55–63 cm. **Weight:** about 20 kg.
Colour: white with brown or orange
patches or with yellow-brown markings
and a brown mantle, but this is not so
desirable.

189

The Pointer is the only short-haired breed of English gundog. Its origin is in Spain, where so-called *perro de punta*, dogs which indicated the presence of game by pointing, were bred since ancient times. Such dogs were brought to England at the beginning of the eighteenth century by British officers who had fought in Spain. The original type was heavier and slower and for that reason English breeders crossed it with Foxhounds and lighter French hounds, thereby developing the present-day Pointer with its excellent nose, swift broad-searching range and steadfast pointing, which works far beyond shotgun range and under no circumstances flushes game before the sports-man arrives at the scene. It is said that the Pointer can scent a partridge at a distance of 500 m. The Pointer is not permitted to bring in downed game in case this might pose a threat to the steadfastness of its pointing. Other dogs, such as the Golden Retriever, were developed for that purpose. Pointers were brought to Europe at the beginning of the nineteenth century but here they are used as multipurpose gundogs.

A good idea of what the Spanish ancestor of the Pointer looked like is provided by the Perdiguero de Burgos, or Spanish Pointer, one of the oldest Spanish breeds of working gundogs which indicates the presence of game by pointing. It is representative of a heavier original type and is used for hunting all kinds of small game.

Extremely popular in Portugal is the closely related Perdigueiro Portugues. It is smaller, lighter and more active; however it is practically unknown outside Portugal.

2 ♂

3 ♂

Pointer
Height: dog 63–69 cm, bitch 61–66 cm.
Weight: 25–30 kg. **Colour:** most often white with yellow, orange, brown (1) or black patches. Also self-coloured dogs in any of the aforesaid colours.

Perdiguero de Burgos
Height: dog 65–75 cm, bitch 62–70 cm.
Weight: 25–30 kg. **Colour:** white with
liver patches (2), or liver with white
patches.

1 ♂

Perdigueiro Portugues
Height: dog 56 cm, bitch 52 cm. **Weight:**
19–24 kg. **Colour:** most often solid
chestnut, also white, yellow (3), reddish
yellow or black. Also allowed are
combinations of the aforesaid colours.

Rough-haired gundogs are very popular because they are hardy and versatile and very willing to work in water. Until recently the various breeds of rough-haired gundogs were frequently crossed and nowadays even experts sometimes find it difficult to determine the breed of a given dog. One of the oldest breeds of rough-haired gundogs developed in Germany is the Deutsch Stichelhaar. Today it is threatened with extinction, having been supplanted by other rough-haired breeds.

At the end of the nineteenth century, a breed was supposed to be developed in Germany to combine a steady point and the willingness to retrieve with work in water. Selected for the purpose were pointers and Poodles, including the now unknown Jagdpudel, and after many difficulties the desired outcome was achieved in the form of the Poodle Pointer. The dogs of the first generation, obtained from the initial breeds, were outstanding, but further generations included specimens that were unsatisfactory. Although the stud book was closed in April 1924 (i.e. only dogs whose father and mother are already listed may be registered in the stud book) the breed is not wholly standardised to this day.

Northern Italy is the home of an interesting and apparently very old breed of rough-haired gundog – the Spinone – considered by many authorities to be the forefather of all rough-haired gundogs. Mention of this breed dates from as far back as the seventeenth century. Later, mainly in the nineteenth century, other breeds of gundogs contributed to the improvement of some of its hunting capabilities so that nowadays the Spinone is an excellent dog for work in uncongenial conditions, chiefly in marshy country.

Deutsch Stichelhaar
Height: 60–66 cm. **Weight:** 30 kg.
Colour: brown and white, grey-brown grizzle, with larger or smaller dark brown patches (1). The eyes are brown.

Poodle Pointer (2)
Height: 60–65 cm. **Weight:** 25–30 kg.
Colour: all shades of brown. Small inconspicuous white marks on the breast are permitted. The eyes are yellow to light yellow-brown.

3

Spinone (3)
Height: 52–68 cm. **Weight:** 30–35 kg.
Colour: white or white with orange or chestnut patches. The eyes are dark yellow to ochre.

2 ♂

1

The first dogs of this type appeared in the early nineteenth century at the Court of Karl Augustus of Weimar. More precise records about their origin are lacking. According to some authorities their forebears must be sought in France, but the German breeder Emil Ilgner claims that these dogs were brought from Bohemia. At the Court of Weimar these unusually coloured gundogs were bred further and their breeding was never substantially influenced by other breeds. Noteworthy characteristics of the Weimaraner are its extraordinary talent for tracking, its keenness and its vigilance. That is why the Weimaraner is often used not only for hunting but also as a service dog. In 1929 dogs of this breed were taken to the United States where they became very popular; at present more than three-quarters of all the dogs of this breed are to be found in the USA.

The coat of Weimaraners may be of two types – short-haired or long-haired. Until recently dogs with different coat types were allowed to mate, but currently efforts are being made to breed each type separately.

Height: dog 61–69 cm, bitch 56–64 cm. **Weight:** 23–28 kg. **Colour:** silver-grey, silver-fawn or mouse-grey, including transitions between these shades (1). The head and ears may be somewhat lighter; sometimes there is a long stripe running along the back. Small white markings on the breast and toes are allowed. The nose is a dark fleshy colour, greyish towards the edges. Pups are grey-blue with azure-blue eyes up until the age of two months (2), from the third month the coat acquires a grey-silver tinge and the eyes become bright amber yellow (3). The final definite colouring of the coat and eyes can be judged only after the pups are eight months old.

The coat of short-haired Weimaraners (5) is short, fine, and thicker than that of other short-haired gundogs. The coat of long-haired Weimaraners (4) is about 3–5 cm long, slightly longer on the breast and belly, with well-feathered thighs and a plumed tail. In the short-haired variety the tail should be docked to 4–4.5 cm when the pups are one or two days old; in the long-haired variety it should be shortened by two or three vertebrae at the age of fourteen days.

2

3

1 ♂

TOY DOGS

Affenpinscher

This is a very ancient breed of small dogs developed in Germany. These dogs were first shown as early as 1434 in paintings by the Flemish painter van Eyck, and later frequently by Albrecht Dürer. The Affenpinscher apparently figured in the origins of the Griffons Belges, but these, however, were developed into a type with protruding forehead and greatly abbreviated muzzle, while the Affenpinscher retained the appearance of the earlier type. Sadly the breed was threatened with extinction at the turn of the century because it was often crossed with the Miniature Schnauzer. At this time even dogs of the same parentage were variously classified according to their teeth: those that had an undershot bite were Affenpinschers, those that had a scissor bite were Miniature Schnauzers. Only very slowly and gradually did German breeders succeed in saving the breed and keeping it pure.

There were also difficulties with coloration and it was 30 years before breeders succeeded in eliminating all undesirable colouring to attain the correct, solid black. Litters included pups coloured black and tan as well as yellow, red, grey, and with markings. Up until 1917 only 40 per cent solid black specimens were registered, but in 1931 the number jumped to 90 per cent and in 1940 to 97 per cent. However, it has only been since 1946 that the number registered has been the desirable 100 per cent.

The Affenpinscher is described as a combination of intrepidness, obstinacy, good humour and droll dignity. It is quick-tempered and, as a watchdog, fiery and ferocious towards all strangers. Towards its owner, however, it is always extremely affectionate.

3   4

Height: 23 cm. **Weight:** a maximum of 4 kg. **Colour:** black (1). The coat on the head is typical of this breed. The hair of the eyebrows and round the eyes is hard and bristly, on the chin, cheeks and top of the head it is hard and long. The coat should give the face a monkey-like expression (2).

The tail may be docked by about three vertebrae, or undocked. The ears can be dropped or held erect (3). In dropped ears the tips fold over in the shape of a letter V (4). At shows primary importance in judging is laid on the overall appearance.

2

1

197

The origin of this breed is the same as that of the King Charles Spaniel. The Cavalier King Charles Spaniel, however, is a representative of an earlier type. At the 1926 Crufts Show, the most famous dog show in Britain, American participants pointed out that the King Charles Spaniels differed markedly from the type depicted in the paintings of the sixteenth, seventeenth and eighteenth centuries. One of the participants, Rosswell Eldridge, even offered £ 25 to any breeder who would revive the old, original type. The British took on this task and two years later saw the setting up of a standard which remains unchanged and valid to the present day. The original type was named the Cavalier King Charles Spaniel. The main difference between it and the King Charles Spaniel is in the shape of the head. The Cavalier King Charles Spaniel has a flat forehead and a longer muzzle with the ridge from the bare of the stop to the tip of the nose measuring about 4 cm in length, whereas the King Charles Spaniel has an arched forehead with the dome extending above the eyes and the ridge of the muzzle so shortened that the space between the eyes and nose forms a hollow just big enough to hold a marble.

The Cavalier King Charles Spaniel has the same characteristics as its more highly bred relative. It is affectionate, playful, a good companion and good with children, bold and extremely attached to its owner. It shows hunting tendencies, with a particularly strong liking for feathered game.

Height: 30–35 cm (height is not definitely prescribed by the standard). **Weight:** 5.4–8.2 kg. **Colouring:** the same four types as for the King Charles Spaniel. Black and tan is glossy black with mahogany markings on the fore-muzzle, above the eyes, on the legs, inside the ears and under the tail. Blenheim (1) is pearly white with chestnut-red patches and a regular pattern on the head. Tricolor (2) is pearly white with black patches and mahogany markings on the cheeks, inside the ears, above the eyes and on the forehead. Ruby is whole-coloured rich red.

1

The coat is long, fine, freely hanging and wavy or slightly curly. The ears are profusely hairy, the legs are feathered and the tail, which may be docked or undocked, has a plume. Care of the coat consists of daily combing and brushing.

Chihuahua

The Chihuahua is the world's tiniest dog (Fig. 3 shows the size of a puppy compared with that of a glass tumbler). Nothing is known about its origins, although reports of such dogs were made by the conquistadores, and further information can be deduced in remnants of the destroyed Aztec culture. It seems that such tiny dogs were the playthings of Aztec princesses and also played an important role in the religious life of the Aztecs. They were considered to be companions of the souls of the dead for all eternity and were therefore sacrificed in funeral rites. Aztec priests kept and bred such dogs, called *techichis,* as far back as the eighth century. These dogs were also raised and kept, however, by ordinary folk – for food. With the fall of Tenochtitlán these small dogs fell into oblivion, but lived on in the villages of Mexican Indians.

In the mid-nineteenth century Indians in the province of Chihuahua started selling these miniature dogs to tourists and so the breed surfaced once again and was given a new name – Chihuahua. They became widespread in the United States but also made their way to Europe, where they have become extremely popular, especially in recent years. The standard for the breed was established in 1942.

The original Chihuahuas were short-haired. Later, in the United States, there appeared a long-haired mutation which became fixed through selective breeding. The Chihuahua is a wary dog which barks at the slightest disturbance. Rather remarkable is its greatly developed hunting instinct.

3

Height: 15–23 cm. **Weight:** 0.9–2.7 kg; usually it ranges between 1.3 and 1.8 kg. **Colour:** All colours and mixtures of colours are allowed. The dogs are generally whitish with dingy yellow markings on the back, flanks and nape, also black and white and tri-coloured. There is often a white blaze and a white patch on the breast. Rare, but highly prized, is a pale grey-blue colouring. The eyes should be black, brown, blue or ruby-red; in light-coloured dogs light eyes are allowed. They are large, round and pronounced but must not be protuberant.

The coat of the short-haired variety
(1) is dense, soft, close-lying and glossy.
In the long-haired variety (2, 3) it is long
and of a soft, smooth texture; there is
a fringe on the ears, a collar on the neck
and the entire tail is hairy.

Chinese Crested Dog and Mexican Hairless Dog

Long before the beginning of the present century there existed in China dogs which were hairless except for a crest on the head, a fringe on the ears, and a tuft of hair on the tip of the tail. As a type, however, they were extremely non-uniform and that is why the British, who set up the standard, divided them into two types: the Deer Type with a slender body, long slender legs and delicate bones, and the Cobby Type, with shorter legs and heavier bones. The breed is thought now to be extinct in China, but elsewhere it has been pure-bred for more than a hundred years.

Hairless dogs may be encountered elsewhere, for instance in some parts of Africa and America. African hairless dogs have not yet received official recognition as a breed, but the American breeds of Xoloitzcuintli and Mexican Hairless Dogs are recognised. Not much is known about their origin, but probably they are native breeds because clay figures of such dogs are often found in Aztec graves. These breeds are relatively rare and are not widely kept or bred. They differ from the Chinese Crested Dog by being more lively and also in the fact that they generally do not bark but whine and howl.

The Chinese Crested Dog is a hardy, undemanding dog which becomes readily acclimatised even to cold conditions. The Mexican Hairless Dog is more delicate. In both breeds greater attention must be paid to dogs with pink skin for they tend to burn more readily when exposed to strong sunlight.

Chinese Crested Dog (1)
Height: 28–33 cm. **Weight:** up to 5.5 kg.
Colour: all colours are permitted, solid or patched in various combinations. The commonest are blue, pink, mauve and golden. In summer the colour is darker than in winter.

2 ♂

Mexican Hairless Dog (2)
Height: about 30 cm. **Weight:** about 5 kg. **Colour:** Here, too, any solid or patched colour is allowed. Commonest are greyish-pink, pink or grey.

It seems that hairless dogs originated as mutation independently of one another in various parts of the world. Besides lack of hair some possess other negative characteristics, e.g. toothlessness (3). The premolars are always absent, the remaining teeth weak. According to detailed studies carried out in recent years, these dogs may lack as many as seventeen teeth.

English Toy Terrier: see p. 114.

The group of small Griffons Belges is a very interesting one. Its forebears included Dutch and German Schnauzers and French Griffons as well as the Pug. Of relatively uniform build, the breed was divided into three varieties differing in colour and coat. Since 1905, when standards were established for all three varieties, the separate types have still not yet become firmly fixed and litters may include pups of different kinds. The Griffon Belge and Griffon Bruxellois are breeds with coarse, shaggy unkempt coats, longer on the chin, cheeks, muzzle and round the eyes. On the chin it forms a beard and the eyebrows are very shaggy. The two breeds differ only in colour. The tail is docked.

Griffons are lively but not restless and make good, vigilant watchdogs. For their size they have immense staying power and enjoy accompanying their owner over long distances.

Breeding is very difficult. The bitch generally has a difficult time whelping and the litters are usually small, often of only one or two pups. Frequently there are faults in the quality and colour of the coat and only a good, experienced breeder with an indefinable 'sixth sense' is rewarded with success. The typical shape of the head, as well as the typical coat, are not acquired until the pups are one and a half years old, which also makes the breeder's task more difficult.

2 ♀

Griffon Belge
Height: 21–28 cm. **Weight:** 2.7–4.5 kg.
Colour: black (1) or black with rusty markings.

Griffon Bruxellois
Height: 21–28 cm. **Weight:** 2.7–4.5 kg.
Colour: red or rusty (2), preferably with a dark mask.

In order to maintain the proper structure of the coat frequent bathing is not advised. The coat should be combed and brushed regularly and the beard may be washed as required. In both breeds the nose, eyelashes and lips must all be black. The eyes are set far apart; they are large, round and protuberant and should be as dark as possible. The feet have black toe pads and black nails.

1 ♀

Japanese Chin (Japanese Spaniel) and Tibetan Spaniel

The origin of the Japanese Chin must be looked for in China. It was the Japanese, however, who developed it and gave it its present-day appearance. Its history may be traced from about the eighth century, when the Japanese Chin was kept and bred at temples as well as by the nobility. The aim was to obtain the smallest possible dogs. Besides the normal breeding procedure, pups were purportedly given saké (an alcoholic drink made from fermented rice) in order to retard their growth. The dogs were carried in bamboo cages or inside the sleeves of kimonos. These miniature dogs were extremely delicate, however, and so later breeding efforts focused on slightly larger types.

The Japanese Chin came to Europe in three different ways. The first time it was brought by missionaries, returning from the Orient, as a gift for Princess Catherine of Braganza, who, in 1662, became the queen of Charles II of England. It was brought again to England in 1860 by Admiral Perry, as a gift for Queen Victoria. On the third occasion, in 1880, it was sent as a gift from the Japanese Empress to Empress Augusta, the wife of German Emperor Wilhelm II. The dogs then became very popular and were subsequently brought to Europe more often.

Without doubt the Japanese Chin's ancestry includes the Tibetan Spaniel, an ancient breed kept and bred in Tibetan monasteries. Similar dogs were said to have been brought to Europe by the Mongols as early as the fifteenth century.

Japanese Chin
Height: the smaller the better. **Weight:** 1.8–3.2 kg. **Colour:** white with clearly defined black (1) or reddish-yellow (2) patches. The coat is soft, silky, straight and long except on the head and the front of the forelegs, where it is short. The tail is profusely hairy and held curled on the back like a chrysanthemum blossom. Dogs with black markings should have a black nose, dogs with reddish-yellow markings may have a dark flesh-coloured nose, but a dark nose is preferable.

Tibetan Spaniel (3)
Height: about 25.4 cm. **Weight:** 4–6.8 kg.
Colour: a wide range is allowed —
golden-yellow, cream, white, yellow,
brown, grey-brown, black, black and tan,
either solid colours or white with large
patches in one of the aforesaid colours,
also tricolour.

3

1

This breed was named after Charles I of England who had a great fondness for these dogs. One of them appears in a picture painted in the seventeenth century by Sir Anthony van Dyck. Up until the nineteenth century this small spaniel, often called the Toy Spaniel, was used to hunt small game, mainly birds, but later it was kept purely as a companion dog. The present-day dog differs from the original type in its smaller size, shorter muzzle and more rounded head. This short-muzzled type did not become widely popular until the nineteenth century and from this period dates the division of the King Charles Spaniel into four types of colouring: black and tan, tricolour, Blenheim and ruby – two of them multicoloured and two self-coloured (black and tan is considered to be self-coloured). Multicoloured and self-coloured types must not be crossed.

The King Charles Spaniel, which has been raised in very close association with people for countless generations, has a naturally affectionate and sweet-tempered disposition. It is very active but not nervous, readily trained, and requires gentle and kind treatment. Despite its small size it is an intrepid watchdog.

4

Height: 26–32 cm. **Weight:** 3.6–6.3 kg. Each of the four types of colouring bears a separate name. Black and tan (1) is glossy black with mahogany markings on the fore-muzzle, above the eyes, on the legs, on the inside of the ears, on the chest and underneath the tail. Ruby (3) is a solid reddish-brown. Blenheim (2) is pearly white with chestnut-red patches. The colouring on the head must be symmetrical. Tricoloured dogs (4) are pearly white with black patches and reddish-brown markings on the cheeks, the inner sides of the ears and above the eyes.

The coat of King Charles Spaniels is profuse, long and silky, lying close to the body if possible, slightly wavy, but under no circumstances curly. There is long feathering on the ears, feathering on the legs and also on the tail, which may be docked if desired. The coat requires daily combing and brushing.

This is an ancient breed of which mention is made by such writers as Pliny and Aristotle. It was called *canis melitensis* because it originated on the Dalmatian island of Melitea, the present-day Yugoslav Mljet. From about the sixteenth century, however, the dog has been called the Maltese, although it has nothing whatever to do with the island of Malta. It was frequently depicted on ancient vases and in ancient paintings. It was a favourite of the ladies of Rome and Athens, who draped it with jewels; Julius Caesar chided Roman women for caring more about their dogs than their children.

The Maltese is sweet-tempered and intelligent and makes a good companion, although it likes to bark. Its coat requires daily combing and brushing.

The Bichon Frisé, or Bichon à Poil Frisé, is closely related to the Maltese. In the fifteenth century it was said to have been brought to France from the Balearic Islands and was often known by the exotic name of Tenériffe. French ladies treated it in much the same way as Roman and Greek women treated the Maltese.

The Lowchen (Little Lion Dog) is recognised as a French breed by the FCI, even though it is known that in the late sixteenth century these dogs were already kept and bred by the Flemish. Its build and the angle of its legs are more reminiscent of Poodles than Bichons. Nowadays this breed is kept only rarely.

2

3

Maltese (1)
Height: not over 25.5 cm. **Weight:** 3–4 kg. **Colour:** pure white with the pink of the skin shining through. The longest hair, measuring 22–30 cm, is on the head (it may be tied with a ribbon); it forms a natural parting on the back. Its texture is soft and silky. The nose, rims of the eyelids, pads of the feet and nails should be black, the eyes are dark ochre.

Bichon Frisé (2)
Height: a maximum of 28 cm. **Weight:**
less than 4 kg. **Colour:** white, darker
colouring of the ears is permissible as
long as they are not too dark.

Lowchen (3)
Height: 20–35 cm. **Weight:** 2.5–3 kg.
Colour: preferably pure white, lemon or
black, but other colours are also
allowed. The coat is trimmed in the 'lion
cut'.

Pinschers are among the oldest of German breeds. Originally they varied in size and also had varied coats but in time the separate types became constant and developed into independent breeds. Rough-haired pinschers gave rise to the Schnauzers, large smooth-haired pinschers gave rise to the Dobermanns, and the smaller smooth-haired pinschers became the Miniature Pinschers.

The development of the Miniature Pinscher was not a simple matter. The original aim was to develop a dog of the smallest possible size and thus the results were often underdeveloped specimens with a rounded skull, protuberant eyes, unstable nerves and constantly quivering bodies. Only patient and consistent selective breeding succeeded in eliminating these faults and obtaining a small dog without any signs of stunted growth, which had steady nerves and was lively, passionate, and wary, in other words a kind of miniature Dobermann. It deservedly became very popular in many countries.

One of the most recent breeds is the Harlequin Pinscher, developed in Germany and officially recognised by the FCI in 1958. It is definitely a companion dog, kept as a pet. Nevertheless there is no mistaking its origin; it is quite good at catching mice and rats and does so enthusiastically if given the chance. Compared with other Pinscher breeds, however, the Harlequin is less hardy.

3 ♂

Miniature Pinscher
Height: 25–30 cm. **Weight:** 3–4 kg.
Colour: various shades of reddish-brown (2), black and tan (1), blue-grey with tan markings, and chocolate-brown with tan markings. The markings, as sharply defined as possible, are located on the cheeks, lips, lower jaw, above the eyes, on the throat, breast, toes and feet, on the inner side of the hind legs and round the anus.

Harlequin Pinscher (3)
Height: 30–35 cm. **Weight:** about 4.5 kg.
Colour: two kinds are permitted: white or grey with black or dark patches and brindle, with or without tan markings.

In both breeds the tail is docked to about three vertebrae. The nose in black Miniature Pinschers and Harlequin Pinschers should always be black, in brown Miniature Pinschers it is brown.

1 ♂

2 ♀

213

Pekingese

According to an old Chinese legend, a lion fell in love with a monkey and their union gave rise to the Pekingese. From the monkey it inherited its beautiful deep eyes and from the lion its calm dignified bearing, courage and mane. For many centuries the Pekingese lived only at the imperial palace in Peking and it could be kept by no one other than the emperor, under threat of death. These dogs were known to be kept at the imperial court as far back as the Tang dynasty in the eighth century.

When the palace was seized in 1860 by British soldiers and the imperial family forced to flee, the empress had all the Pekingese killed so that they would not fall into the hands of the 'white devils'. Five of these dogs, however, escaped this dire fate by hiding behind curtains and these were taken to England by British officers. Four went to the Duchess of Richmond and one bitch was presented as a gift to Queen Victoria. The bitch was given the name Looty and we know exactly what she looked like. The Queen had her portrait painted by the painter Landseer and this picture now hangs in Windsor Castle. Following her death, Looty was given to the Natural History Museum in London, where she is on permanent display as a preserved, stuffed and mounted exhibit.

From this display we know that the Pekingese of that time differed from the Pekingese of today. The present type is the result of selective breeding by British breeders. All Pekingese are descended from those first five dogs. Their descendants were taken back to China again, but not until after the First World War.

Pekingese dogs vary markedly in character, but all remain playful well into advaced age.

2   ♀

♂

Height: 15–25 cm; smaller dogs are more highly prized but under no circumstances should the typical appearance be affected by its small size.**Weight:** not over 5.5 kg. **Colour:** all colours except albino and liver. All solid colours (3) may be various shades of brindle or may have white markings; a black mask (1) is desirable. In multicoloured dogs white must be the predominating colour; coloured markings should be symmetrical and there should be a white blaze on the head.

A typical feature of the Pekingese is its face (2), which is broad and well wrinkled. The nose should be short and broad and set well between the eyes. The cheeks should not cave in beneath the eyes.

3

1 ♂

Dutch sailors are said to have brought back from the Far East small dogs, with the facial part of the skull greatly shortened (2), which looked like short-haired Pekingese. Similar dogs, apparently forebears of the present-day Pug, appear in fifteenth-century paintings. They came to England from Holland during the reign of William and Mary and became very popular. The Pug was depicted in numerous paintings, in the form of statuettes produced by many of the porcelain works of Europe, and its head adorned the tops of walking sticks as well as the stoppers of perfume bottles. This fashion, however, ended in the late nineteenth century and the Pug slowly fell into oblivion. Its place was taken by other, mostly long-haired breeds. Nevertheless, there remained breeders who continued to breed Pugs because of their intelligence, playfulness and liveliness. Only recently is their popularity once again on the rise, although they are still one of the less common breeds. The origin of the breed's name is the subject of several theories. In the English language it is relatively clear, for the word 'pug' is the slang term for a boxer or pugilist. In the German language its name – Mops – is derived from the south German *moppen, moppern* or *möpen* meaning to grimace, in other words referring to the dog's dejected (moping) facial expression.

The Brabançon, sometimes also called the Petit Brabançon, belongs to the group of Griffons Belges, but its development was markedly influenced by the Pug, from which, among other things, it also inherited its short coat. At first these short-haired dogs were not popular; they were considered an unwelcome mutation which appeared in litters of rough-haired griffons. However, as early as 1880 they were shown in Brussels and in 1905 they received a standard of their own. They are wary watchdogs and pleasant companions.

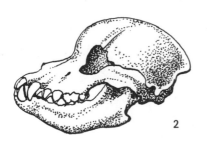

2

Pug
Height: 30–35 cm. **Weight:** 6.4–8.2 kg.
Colour: silver (1), fawn, apricot or black.
The fore-muzzle, ears, spots on the cheeks, on the forehead and the stripe on the back must be clearly defined and as black as possible.

Brabançon
Height: 21–28 cm. **Weight:** 2.7–4.5 kg.
Colour: red, with or without a black mask (3). The tail is docked to two-thirds of its length.

Yorkshire Terrier, Silky Terrier and Australian Terrier

The breed was developed in the mid-nineteenth century in Yorkshire. The purpose for which these dogs were intended was to kill mice and rats in the homes of labourers and artisans who often lived in very cramped and sometimes squalid conditions. Used in its development were small long-haired terriers, the Skye Terrier, Dandie Dinmont Terrier and the Maltese. The Yorkshire Terrier is lively, happy and courageous and a good watchdog. Its coat, which is long and silky, requires regular care. The pups are born with a short black coat with rust-coloured markings. The lovely long coat does not grow in until some time between the second and third year but the typical colouring appears earlier, round about the first year. Few Yorkshire Terriers have a coat of show condition before their third year.

The Yorkshire Terrier figured in the development of two interesting Australian breeds. The first is the Silky Terrier, previously also called the Sydney-Silky. It was developed in Australia at the turn of the century but did not receive official recognition until 1959. Other breeds which figured in its development, besides the Yorkshire Terrier, were the Skye Terrier, Scottish Terrier and the Maltese.

The second Australian breed is the Australian Terrier, whose ancestry also included the Cairn Terrier. This breed is still in the process of development and is relatively non-uniform in the various breeding kennels, although its first standard was set up as far back as 1921. The Australian Terrier became very popular in Asia; in India, for example, it is widely kept as a companion dog.

2

Yorkshire Terrier (1)
Height: 20–24 cm. **Weight:** 1.5–3.2 kg.
Colour: dark steel-blue from the back of the head to the root of the tail, tan on the breast, head and legs, with the colouring on the sides of the head, the nose and the ears a darker hue. The tail is docked to medium length.

Silky Terrier (2)
Height: 20–25 cm. **Weight:** 3–4.5 kg.
Colour: blue or blue-grey with red to liver markings. The top of the head is silvery, the remainder of the head and the ears golden-red, the legs golden-red to tan, the back and flanks blue, the tail a rich blue. It is important that the colours are correctly distributed.

Australian Terrier (3)
Height: 24–25 cm. **Weight:** 6.3 kg.
Colour: blue is preferred, but also
permitted are black, grey, sandy to red,
with or without tan markings on the
head and legs. The markings should be
as dark as possible, and the tuft of hair
between the ears should be blue, sandy
or tan.

3

1

INDEX

(numbers in bold refer to main entries)

221